# GET READY.
# GET SET. GO!

2015

Get Ready. Get Set. Go! - MBA/Graduate Edition

© 2014 WhiteStar Enterprises Inc. All rights reserved.

For information on getting permission for excerpts, contact readysetgobook@gmail.com.

ISBN-13: 978-0692241967 (WhiteStar Enterprises Inc)
ISBN-10: 0692241965

BY WILLIAM J. WHITE

# DEDICATION

*This book is dedicated to my
wonderful wife Jane, who died in a tragic
accident on December 28, 2012.
Her faith, love, and inspiration filled
my life for over fifty two years.*

# CONTENTS

Foreword      11
Acknowledgments      13
About the Author      15
Introduction: Launching Your Extraordinary Career      17

## PART I: GET READY      23

### WHO YOU ARE      25

Assessing Emotional Intelligence
Understanding Emotional Undercurrents
Receiving and Using Feedback
Tips and Takeaways

### WHAT YOU KNOW      33

Taking a First Step Toward Your Dream
A Caveat on Dreams
Tips and Takeaways

### HOW YOU WORK WITH OTHERS      37

Who's on Your Team?
Beware the Resistors
Where Can You Be at Your Best?
Now You're Ready
Tips and Takeaways

### GET READY : PLANNING WORKSHEET      43

## PART II: GET SET     45

### WHO YOU ARE     47

Imagining Your First Days
Updating Your Image
Tips and Takeaways

### WHAT YOU KNOW     52

Educating Yourself to "Get Set"
Knowing Where You Can Make a Difference
Tips and Takeaways

### HOW YOU WORK WITH OTHERS     57

Communication Style: It's All About Your Boss
Have a "Get Set" Conversation
Develop a Team Mindset
Tips and Takeaways

### GET SET : PLANNING WORKSHEET     65


## PART III: GO     67

### WHO YOU ARE     69

It Starts with a Smile
The Network Beyond Your Cubicle
Be Resilient
Tips and Takeaways

### WHAT YOU KNOW     77

Tips and Takeaways

**HOW YOU WORK WITH OTHERS**                                                            **82**

    Your First Boss
    Taking on More Work—Especially Jobs No One Else Wants
    Don't Get Distracted
    Group Dynamics
    Who Knows Who Knows Whom?
    Ethical Dilemmas
    Look for Mentors
    Tips and Takeaways

**GO! : PLANNING WORKSHEET**                                              **95**

*Appendix: Personal Onboarding Plans*                                    *97*
*Resources*                                                                                          *122*

*FOREWORD*

## "BY FAILING TO PREPARE, YOU ARE PREPARING TO FAIL."
### —BENJAMIN FRANKLIN

**YESTERDAY,** I attended—as a spectator—the Arizona Ironman triathlon in Tempe, Arizona. I was there because our younger daughter was one of the athletes. It was her first ultra-distance triathlon. It began with a 2.4 mile swim in the Tempe Town Lake followed by a 112 mile bike ride and a 26.2 mile marathon run. There were 1,958 males and 749 females participating. They ranged in age from 18 to 72 and they came from 45 different countries. They had entered the event for a variety of reasons. About 75 were professionals competing for the top prizes and qualifying for more select Ironman competitions elsewhere. Most were experienced competitors who were hoping to set personal best times on the fast Tempe course. Some entered as an incentive for their family and friends to contribute funds to important charitable causes, and there were about 900 first time triathletes who were there to have the experience of pushing themselves beyond their limits and to see if they could, in the words of the 1976 Rocky film, "go the distance".

Despite all of the differences among those Ironman athletes, they had one thing in common: EXTENSIVE PREPARATION. You don't succeed in this sort of punishing physical and mental challenge without rigorous training and a strict nutritional program to prepare your body for an extreme and intensive effort. You need to push yourself in practice in order to increase your endurance and your tolerance for the pain that you will feel during each segment of the event, and you need to develop the mental toughness and the confidence to continue the race no matter what happens.

For most meaningful human endeavors, preparation is the prerequisite to performance and success. The best musicians, sports teams, students, teachers, and people in a wide variety of organizations and activities prepare themselves extensively so that they can do their best when the chips are down. "Practice makes perfect" is not just a cliché. It's a truth. In his book, *Outliers*, Malcolm

Gladwell points out that those who become superstars in various fields aren't just talented flukes. They succeed because they systematically—often because of special circumstances—have far more time-on-task experience, guidance, and motivation to hone their skills. In short, they are better prepared.

Bill White has taken the concept of preparation into an area where it is usually not applied: Preparing yourself for a new work assignment—a new job—in advance of joining the organization. This can be a first job out of school, but it can also be a new opportunity for you in the same or a different organization as you progress in your career. Of course, many established companies have onboarding programs for new employees. However, even for new jobs in those companies, Bill's "Ready, Set, Go" approach can enable you to contribute sooner and to advance your career faster. More importantly, many of the most exciting job opportunities these days are in young, entrepreneurial companies that are hiring rapidly and often just taking a "sink-or-swim" approach with new employees. Preparing yourself fully for your first days on the job in such organizations and following Bill's advice for contributing more than is expected as a committed team player (e.g., volunteering for work that needs doing and lacks doers) can enable you to make a bigger, positive difference and to become a highly valued employee sooner.

I have known and worked with Bill White for more than fifteen years. We have served on two company Boards together. One was the Board of a large, established public company, and the other is the Board of a young high-technology startup. Moreover, we have both offered similar courses that help to prepare college students for building enterprises and for living productive lives—he at Northwestern and I at Princeton. I have been impressed with Bill's commitment to his students and to their successes. Moreover, I have admired the solid values that he has instilled by his personal example, by his guidance for his students, and for whomever he is engaged for a variety of activities and groups. This book—*Get Ready. Get Set. Go!*—is not just about preparing yourself to make your best contribution in a new work assignment. It's about doing so in a manner that will benefit others inside and outside of that organization based on your work approach and your values.

OK… it's time for you to enjoy the book and where it will lead. Then, you'll be prepared for what comes next.

*November 18, 2013*

—Ed Zschau
*Business executive, Professor and former U.S. Congressman*

# ACKNOWLEDGEMENTS

This book is the result of several insightful requests. Ed Zschau, of Princeton University, asked if there was a simple onboarding brochure for students starting their careers. Other folks asked me for a "Cliff Notes" version of "From Day One", my original book dealing with the issues a young graduate faces starting a career.

Further, a number of my students asked me how they might better spend the time between accepting a job offer and their actual starting date.

The more I thought about these requests, the more I became convinced there was a need to write this book.

My thanks go to each of my hundreds of students who over the last year have read and reacted to versions, chapters, graphics, and checklists for the book. They provided an invaluable positive contribution.

One of the fun aspects of putting the book together was working with my illustrator, Mia McNary, who also happens to be my daughter. A professional artist and entrepreneur, she shares her love of art and art education in her school, for special causes, and with her friends. She created the cover art and the inside illustrations.

Tricia Crisafulli and I have now collaborated on two books. She has the special talent of listening to my thoughts and ideas and creating a document that many have said sounds like me talking and is easy to read. When she says, "I like that story", I know we are on target. She had a special positive impact on this book.

Much gratitude goes to Kelli Christiansen as the careful editor who provided great feedback and polished these pages.

The book was brought to life by the team at Ross/Madrid. Their fresh, creative approach to the entire look and layout of the book resulted in a feeling of excitement which immediately draws the reader's attention. Robert Ross and Roland Madrid have made a fabulous contribution to the positioning of the book. For this, I am tremendously appreciative. Not only are they unusually creative, they are fun and easy to work with. My deepest thanks to them.

# ABOUT THE AUTHOR

**F**OLLOWING MORE THAN THIRTY YEARS OF SUCCESS in the business world and ultimately serving as chairman and CEO of a NYSE company, William J. White has spent the past fifteen years teaching and advising students on their careers as a professor at Northwestern University. White's research focuses on what makes a successful transition to a new position: the onboarding process.

A popular speaker and the author of *From Day One*, a career guide targeted to young graduates, White has been recognized as an outstanding teacher at Northwestern and at its McCormick School of Engineering and Applied Science.

In addition to serving on numerous public company boards, he has been a director of multiple private and nonprofit organizations. Some of those include Reader's Digest Association, USG Corporation, and Bell & Howell Company, where he also served as Chairman and CEO. White is a life trustee of Northwestern University, NorthShore University Healthsystem, and the Field Museum of Chicago.

White is an Industrial Engineering graduate of Northwestern University, and he received an MBA degree from Harvard University.

He lives on Chicago's Northshore. He has four children and thirteen grandchildren.

# INTRODUCTION

## LAUNCHING YOUR EXTRAORDINARY CAREER

**Y****OU'VE RECENTLY GRADUATED** or you're about to—and a new job is on your horizon. Congratulations! You are about to launch an extraordinary career.

Chances are, however, there is a gap—whether spanning weeks or months—between when you accepted a job offer and your first day on the job. The reason is that the timeline for students graduating and starting a job has

# INTRODUCTION
## LAUNCHING YOUR EXTRAORDINARY CAREER

changed dramatically. It wasn't that many years ago when students interviewed for positions and then accepted a job offer in February or March, sometimes as late as April, with a start date of June or July. Now, as we've seen at Northwestern University, where I am a professor of organizational behavior in the school of engineering, graduating seniors are being made offers as early as Thanksgiving but are not going to work until the following August, or even as late as September or October. In other words, there can be a nine to eleven month gap between job acceptance and the first day of employment.

Several factors are contributing to this shift in timing. First, there is increased competition for good students, which means employers are recruiting on campuses earlier. Second, students are more inclined to take one or two months off after graduation to travel or decompress after the rigors of their studies. Third, in the aftermath of the recession of 2008–09, many companies have had to postpone hiring and push back reporting dates to balance out their workforce needs. Because they over-recruited in the past, some have even moved reporting dates as far back as the January after graduation. (In some rare instances, employers are giving their recruits half pay during that gap to keep them committed, even though they are not working.) How are you going to put your gap time to good use?

You should view these weeks or months as more than just "down time." Rather, this interim period is an opportunity to invest in self-assessment and preparation in order to launch your career. The more you do to educate and prepare yourself, the more successful a transition or onboarding experience you're likely to have. That could mean the critical difference between just starting a job and launching an extraordinary career.

In addition, by using this period wisely, you will build healthy habits for future promotions. U.S. Bureau of Labor Statistics data show that the average job tenure for twenty-four to twenty-seven-year-olds is about three years. Extrapolating this out to age sixty-five means you could very well have about a dozen job changes during the course of your professional life. With some job

# INTRODUCTION
## LAUNCHING YOUR EXTRAORDINARY CAREER

changes, you may have a gap of only a few weeks; others could span several weeks or months—or longer. The more you approach these transitions as opportunities for self-assessment and education, the more successful you'll be. That's where this book comes in.

This book is divided into three sections, each designed to take you through a specific period of your preparation time for an extraordinary transition, which typically spans the first six to twelve months after you start. In Part I: Get Ready, you will begin your initial preparation, with a strong focus on yourself, including your strengths and weaknesses, gaps in your knowledge, and what you can do to get yourself ready for your new job. In Part II: Get Set, you will look more closely at the specifics of your new job, from doing thorough research about your employer to having a "Get Set" conversation with your new boss about your responsibilities and the people you should meet. In Part III: Go, you will devise a plan for your initial days and weeks on the job, the impression you make with your new coworkers, and how you can demonstrate that you are a team player.

A worksheet following each part will guide you quickly and visibly through the specific action steps needed to develop and implement your personal onboarding plan. In the Appendix, you will find several examples of actual personal onboarding plans, which will allow you to see how graduates like you have used this book to prepare their individual plans.

Your onboarding should be a proactive process that requires your full participation. In addition to the orientation, training, and other preparation that your company provides, you should take it upon yourself to do your own onboarding, with a special emphasis on self-assessment, from attitude to aptitude. Research has shown that the more successful your onboarding, the bigger

# INTRODUCTION
## LAUNCHING YOUR EXTRAORDINARY CAREER

the head start you'll gain on achieving career success. A quick review of the chart on the next page portrays the more than forty percent reduction in the time it takes to reach proficiency by being a high performing transitioning leader compared to an average transitioning leader. Therefore, you'll want to make sure yours is an extraordinary onboarding trajectory—a learning and experience curve that will help you become a strong contributor months earlier than your colleagues and, potentially, will help you become eligible for a promotion that much sooner. If you can hit the ground running in all your future transitions, think what a difference it could make in your overall career success.

To realize these objectives, you will need to take specific steps. First, you will need to make the effort and execute your own written plan. This will give you a competitive edge versus merely showing up on the first day without having planned ahead to prepare yourself. Then you'll be off and running instead of being stalled at the starting gate.

With that, it's time to get ready ... get set ... go! ☀

# INTRODUCTION
## LAUNCHING YOUR EXTRAORDINARY CAREER

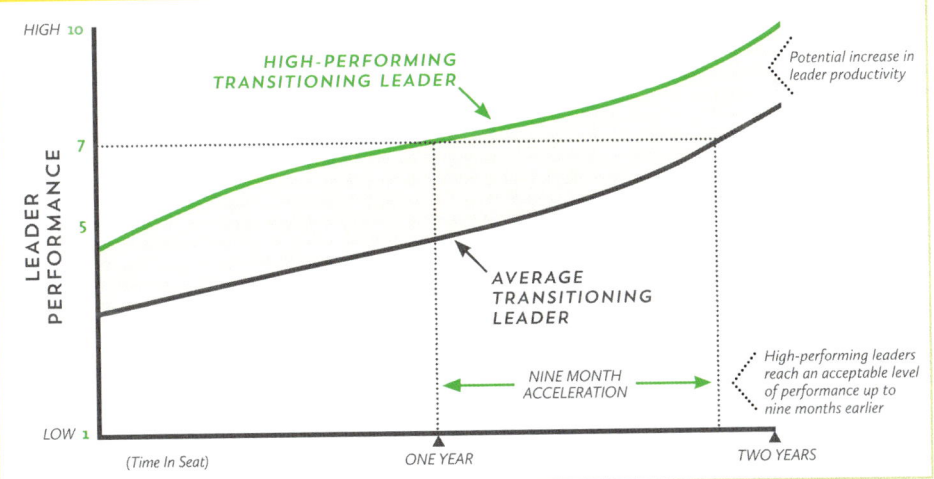

SOURCE: *CEB, Leadership Transition Series — Volume III, Arlington, CA 2005, page 93.*

"BEFORE EVERYTHING ELSE, GETTING READY IS THE SECRET OF SUCCESS."
—HENRY FORD

## PART I

# GET READY.

**THE FIRST STEP** in any endeavor is to get ready for it. Your new job is no exception. The better prepared you are at the start, the more success and satisfaction you're likely to experience throughout the process. Yet often when I speak with my students or young professionals who are entering the workforce, the reaction is "Sure, I'm preparing," or "Oh, I've done that." Just thinking about getting ready, however, isn't really preparing. To be effective, your preparation plan must be in writing. If you don't have a formal plan, how will you know what action steps to take? How will you keep track of your progress? The better your plan, the better your results.

Another value of having a plan is that it allows you to anticipate issues and situations, both positive and negative. The more deliberate you are in your preparation, including by rehearsing scenarios (even with yourself), the more easily you'll overcome setbacks and take advantage of opportunities. As noted in a recent Harvard Business Review article, "a small investment of time and

## PART I

### GET READY

effort upfront can make the difference between simply getting by and truly excelling, between a dead-end move and stepping stone to bigger and better things."[1] With that, let's begin.

At this point, you've successfully completed your job search. Over the past several months, you have probably interviewed multiple times and with several companies, and you narrowed your choices down to one or two opportunities. After the final interview, an offer was made and you accepted.

It's understandable that landing a job is accompanied by a sigh of relief. The worry and wonder, excitement, and anxiety are behind you. Often, the reaction at this point is to say to yourself, "Whew! That's over"—especially if your start date is several months in the future. Don't fall into the trap of thinking that this gap means you have nothing to do. The more time you have until your start date, the more thoroughly you can prepare yourself.

Getting ready opens doors and helps you walk through them. As you devote time and effort to your preparation, you will set realistic expectations while you discover all that you bring to your new employer as an eager contributor and as an enthusiastic new member of the team. ✺

**PART I**

GET READY: WHO YOU ARE

# WHO YOU ARE

**MOST THINGS YOU READ SAY** "it's not about you;" this initial part of the process, however, is all about you. So let's take a step back. You didn't walk into your job interview right from the beach, wearing shorts and an old, faded t-shirt. Properly dressed in business attire, you made a good impression. Now you're going to look into another kind of mirror, one that reflects your performance, your attitude, and your willingness to learn. Professor Laura Morgan Roberts, in an interview with *Working Knowledge*, a newsletter from Harvard Business School, stressed the importance of creating a positive professional image. "People are constantly observing your behavior and forming theories about your competence, character, and commitment, which are rapidly disseminated throughout your workplace."[2]

# PART I
## GET READY: WHO YOU ARE

As you get ready for your new job, it's time to take a look in the mirror of self-assessment, which will help you make a positive first—and lasting—impression.

## ASSESSING EMOTIONAL INTELLIGENCE

▶ **THROUGH YOUR YEARS IN SCHOOL,** internships, and in your earlier positions, you developed many personal skills and habits, encompassing such things as work ethic, a sense of responsibility, cooperation and collaboration with others, and the ability to get the job done. A key component of your success is emotional intelligence: your ability to read people, to detect and navigate the emotional undercurrents of a situation, and to master your emotions.

If you haven't done so already, use the time getting ready for your new job to form a habit of looking for signals and signs, such as body language and facial expressions, which alert you to how people react to you. People's perceptions are reality to them. Assuming you employed your emotional intelligence as you made your job choice, you now have the opportunity to be more deliberate in your efforts until self awareness of your social behaviors becomes second nature. This is a valuable skill you'll use in all of your onboarding assignments—and throughout your career.

Daniel Goleman, author of *Emotional Intelligence*, found that top performers possess both emotional intelligence and cognitive skills. As you advance professionally and deal with more people-related issues rather than technical challenges, emotional intelligence becomes even more important, so it's a good idea to work on it early in your career. Here are some factors to consider as you assess your emotional intelligence:

- How do you handle delayed gratification, which is one of the key elements of emotional intelligence? (Goleman reported on studies of

# PART I
## GET READY: WHO YOU ARE

preschool children who could forgo the instant pleasure of a marshmallow, and linked this ability with future success.)
• Can you think of an example of when you showed your ability to work for a reward that came later (e.g. learning a new computer language, filling in for a colleague without getting paid for it)?
• How can you further develop this skill as you become more mindful of the tradeoffs that result from the choices you make (e.g., taking a lower-paying job now to learn more skills that will lead to better opportunities in the future)?

## UNDERSTANDING EMOTIONAL UNDERCURRENTS

▶ **YOU DON'T NEED TO BE A MIND READER** to have a pretty good idea of what people are thinking and feeling. All you need is the ability to read others' emotions. For some people, this skill comes quite naturally; for others, it takes practice. For all of us, awareness can lead to greater competence.

A fun exercise to strengthen your awareness of facial expressions and body language can be done with the simple activity of watching a day time drama

# PART I
## GET READY: WHO YOU ARE

with the sound turned off. Real life, however, usually is not as emotive as a soap opera. People often cloak their emotions, particularly if there are political stakes involved, which are common in the workplace. This means picking up on subtle cues and nuances. The more skilled you become at reading emotions, the more competent you will become at understanding the undercurrents of group dynamics. As you practice honing your emotional intelligence, ask yourself these questions:

- When have you witnessed or been involved in a politically charged situation in which emotions were hidden? What clues did you pick up?
- Think about mastery of your emotions. Do you lose your temper easily and frequently? In an emotionally charged situation, do you let your emotions get the best of you? Does your body betray your emotions with a racing pulse, flushing face, or sweaty palms? Or, are you able to stay cool and objective and retain your composure?
- What do others say about your reactions under stress? Do you come across as flustered and overheated, or are you too laid back? Awareness of how you are perceived is the first step to managing your emotions, which is a key element of emotional intelligence.

## RECEIVING AND USING FEEDBACK

▶ **AN ASPIRING ACTRESS WAS IN A THEATER** practicing her lines as Lady Macbeth. She didn't notice that the director had been seated in the back until he approached her after the scene.

"May I give you some feedback?" the director asked.

"Certainly," the actress replied. "As long as you tell me how fabulous I am."

Many of us approach feedback the same way: we like to hear what we're good at, but cringe at the thought of hearing something critical, even when it's constructive.

# PART I
## GET READY: WHO YOU ARE

If the word "feedback" makes you groan, it's time for a new attitude. Feedback is a gift that fosters self-awareness. Chances are you've received this gift many times in the past. As you reflect on those occasions when you've been given constructive feedback, what was your reaction? Did you look for ways to put these observations into practice? Or did you set it aside? Your previous attitude toward feedback will color how well you receive others' observations, advice, and suggested actions in the future.

- Do you see feedback as a gift or as something to be endured—or even avoided at all costs?
- Do you find it difficult to ask for feedback because you don't like to hear criticism? Start by seeking the advice, observations, and guidance of someone who cares about you and has your best interest at heart.
- Based on the feedback you have received, how can you put together a plan to reduce your weaknesses and build your strengths?
- What is your attitude toward self-improvement? Are you caught up in perfectionism, or do you seek to become a well-rounded person?
- How have you acted on feedback in the past, based on the suggestions and observations of others? Are you willing to close that loop by revisiting these people to show the progress that you've made and to seek further feedback?

One common piece of feedback relates to listening. There are two kinds of listening. One type is when we pay attention and absorb what is being said. The other is when we wait for the speaker to take a breath so we can jump in with what we have to say. To be successful in your new job, you will need to maximize the first type of listening and minimize the second.

One of my students, Jason, seemed eager to talk to me when he spotted me in the hallway one Monday morning. "Professor White," he said enthusiastically, "how was your weekend?"

I thanked him for asking and recounted a few of the activities I had enjoyed

# PART I

## GET READY: WHO YOU ARE

with my family. For the thirty seconds that I spoke, however, I was aware that Jason did not stand still and had trouble making eye contact. "So how are you, Jason?" I asked.

"Terrific! Let me tell you what happened to me this weekend..."

As Jason launched into his account, I realized that he wasn't at all interested in my weekend. He had merely used that as an opening so he could tell me about what had happened to him. Moral of the story: When someone else speaks, listen. It not only shows respect, but you just might learn something. When you listen, use curious questions (e.g., "Can you tell me more about that?") to demonstrate that you truly are interested in the person's answer. As you become a good listener, you will distinguish yourself because few do it well. If you demonstrate excellent listening skills, you will be unique—and others will notice.

# PART I
## GET READY: WHO YOU ARE

## TIPS AND TAKEAWAYS

→ **Emotional intelligence complements your cognitive skills and helps you stay attuned to others' feelings, thoughts, and perceptions.**

→ **Be aware of your own emotions, particularly how you react to stressful or politically charged situations.**

→ **Think back to the feedback you have received. As it applies to you today, put it into action.**

→ **Feedback is a gift. Knowing how others experience you and perceive your strengths and weaknesses will help you tremendously.**

→ **Refine your listening skills. The rule of thumb is to listen 80 percent of the time and to speak 20 percent of the time.**

Remember, getting ready is meant to be the start of a process that will establish and advance your career. As Peter Drucker observed in his book *Managing Oneself*, "Stay alert and mentally engaged." It's all about you—your strengths, your skills, your experience—and the contribution you will make to your new employer. Self-assessment is critical. ✺

# NOTES

## PART I
### GET READY

# WHAT YOU KNOW

**NOW THAT WE'VE LOOKED AT WHO YOU ARE,** let's switch gears to what you know. As you explore your competencies in light of what may be new career goals, don't lose sight of your personal preferences. Even if you're good at accounting, it may not be the ideal fit if your personality is more suited to working in a creative field. The more you understand yourself and your strengths, the better you can flourish in your new work environment. (A number of online tools can help you, such as www.humanmetrics.com, which offers free self-assessments similar to Myers Briggs.)

As you look at what you know, be aware of intellectual arrogance: believing that the areas in which you are strongest or highly skilled are the most important, whereas those in which you are not as competent are not as important. If you are qualitative by nature, you may not value the "quants." Your blind spots have more to teach you about yourself than your strengths. It's all about awareness—what you know and what you don't know. By admitting to yourself what you need to learn, you'll take a major step forward toward career success.

# PART I
## GET READY: WHAT YOU KNOW

### *TAKING A FIRST STEP TOWARD YOUR DREAM*

▶ **AS YOU START YOUR NEW JOB,** it's not too early to consider how it will advance you toward your longer-term aspirations. Think of your life (professionally and personally) as a mosaic composed of many experiences, opportunities, and lessons learned along the way. When you started out, there were more gaps than filled-in spaces. No matter. With each job and new assignment, you have taken one step closer to where you ultimately want to be.

In your initial assignment, you may be rotated through departments. This will allow both you and the company to find the best match for your aptitudes and their needs. As you get ready, you need to confirm the type of position you'd eventually like to have and where you can exhibit your leadership. For example:

- Do you want to be a consultant and work in a service area, or are you interested in making a product? Is your dream to become a writer or an artist? Are you called to work for a nongovernmental organization (NGO) (e.g., Save the Children or the Peace Corps) or another service organization? Do you want to join the military?
- How can you further refine your vision? For example, if you are interested in making a product, are you more inclined to consumer or industry goods? If you want to work for an NGO, do you see yourself working domestically or on another continent? Do you see yourself analyzing and recommending, or making decisions and taking actions?

> **HOW CAN YOU FURTHER REFINE YOUR VISION?**

# PART I
## GET READY: WHAT YOU KNOW

• Is money driving your decision? Research has shown that money is not a primary driver of satisfaction.

## A CAVEAT ON DREAMS

➤ **IT'S GOOD TO HAVE DREAMS**—we can all agree with that. Dreams inspire us and help us to consider the range of possibilities for ourselves. But sometimes dreams remain just that—dreams. Comedian Stephen Colbert, in his graduation address to the Northwestern University Class of 2011, brought the point home in a very humorous way: "If we all stuck with our first dream," he quipped, "the world would be overrun with cowboys and princesses!" Look beyond the specifics of the dream to see where your passions and interests might lead you. As Colbert observed, when you pursue those things you love, you will ultimately become passionate about them.

Consider Rob, an MBA graduate who took a job with a major consulting company, which had appealed to him for its fast-paced environment and its variety of assignments. While working with one client, Rob became more involved in social networking. Here was his true passion, he realized, and he immediately began building his technical skills in this area.

Pursuing your dream is a step-by-step process, not a giant leap. As you progress, your dream will unfold and may move in new directions.

• As you pursue your dreams, where might they lead you, provided you remain open-minded and flexible?

• What "Plan B" ideas have you considered that might be worth more serious consideration?

# PART I
## GET READY: WHAT YOU KNOW

### TIPS AND TAKEAWAYS

→ Connect the dots between your new job and your dream of where you want to be one day. Can you see how the path might unfold for you?

→ Hold fast to your dreams, but remain flexible in how they might materialize. The pursuit of your ideal position may take you into interesting, alternative opportunities that you never considered before.

→ Keep your focus on the here-and-now, but don't lose sight of the bigger picture—the mosaic that will emerge through all of your experiences and opportunities over a lifetime.

Know what you know—and what you don't know. Focusing on your strengths will give you confidence as you get ready, while identifying your weaknesses and areas of development will help you become better prepared for new opportunities to learn and challenge yourself. ☀

*PART I*

GET READY

# HOW YOU WORK WITH OTHERS

**A**  **CHIEVING AN EXTRAORDINARY TRANSITION** requires a team that includes your new boss, your old one if available, and your colleagues. Getting ready is not a solitary effort. You also have a team of people who are on your side: friends, family, and others who are close to you. Among them are a few key players: the trusted advisors on whom you can rely to give you honest feedback and unbiased advice, particularly on how you interact with others.

You've already been a part of teams, whether in college or as part of a sport or even a hobby. In your earlier job(s), you were not only part of teams, but you may very well have managed teams. As you think about these experiences, con-

# PART I
## GET READY: HOW YOU WORK WITH OTHERS

sider what you were good at and what you enjoyed most. Were you the group leader? Did you act as a leader informally? What did you like about working with others and coordinating activities? Pondering these experiences gives you insight into participating in and managing teams. In addition, an exemplary team member is often a leader in training.

## WHO'S ON YOUR TEAM?

➤ **EVERYONE NEEDS TRUSTED ADVISORS,** the people who have your best interest at heart and who see your potential. Ultimately, your advisors may be your spouse or someone else who is very close to you, but earlier in your life, they will probably be family members or long-time friends. In addition to trusted advisors, you should gather a team of people on whom you can rely for information, introductions, feedback, and a host of other issues. It's time for you to make a list of the people on your team. There may be untapped resources in your circle who are ready and willing to help you.

- Among your undergraduate classmates and MBA associates, to whom have you reached out in the past? Have any of your professors offered to be an advisor or resource to you after graduation? Among your fellow students, which true friends are sounding boards who will give you advice in confidence?
- Among your family members, to whom have you turned for advice? Think beyond your immediate family to extended relatives, such as cousins or a sister-in-law or brother-in-law who is a bit older and has more professional experience.
- Who do your parents or other family members know who could be recruited to your team? For example, does your cousin know someone who works in a field in which you are interested? When someone is one or two steps removed from your inner circle, there is no

## PART I
### GET READY: HOW YOU WORK WITH OTHERS

emotional attachment, so they can be more objective with you. Do your former managers and colleagues have a special viewpoint on your strengths and weaknesses and on your potential to expand your career?

# BEWARE THE RESISTORS

▶ **DURING THE COURSE OF YOUR LIFE,** you'll find that there are people who, well-intentioned though they may be, aren't really part of your team. That's not to say they don't care about you. Often, they just can't see beyond their own self-interests, ideas, and concerns to view you and your life choices clearly. They are the resistors who dig in their heels and put on the blinders where you are concerned. They may include:

**1.** Resentful corporate colleagues—As an MBA, you may have been hired into a job that typically went to a more experienced employee. The "old guard" may be resentful and feel you haven't earned it. They may believe that one of their own or one of their good friends was more deserving of the job but was passed over in your favor. First of all, remember that the decision to hire you for the job was someone else's call. Second, know that the only way to offset this resentment is with exceptional performance.

# PART I
## GET READY: HOW YOU WORK WITH OTHERS

**2.** Clingy boyfriends and girlfriends—Your job offer is in one place and he or she is headed in another direction. When the answer is immediately, "You can't go!" you need to move forward carefully in terms of both the career opportunity and the relationship. Don't make a choice about either that you might regret later.

**3.** Overbearing mentors—Sometimes even an advisor can get a little too ego-invested in your choices. If this person is truly a trusted advisor, then once you explain the rationale for your plans, he or she should get on board and support you. If not, then this person isn't really a trusted advisor.

When you are able to identify your resistors, you become more discerning about their feedback and advice—without damaging your relationships with them. Instead of shutting them down or getting defensive, you are simply able to listen with more emotional intelligence, seeing clearly where their best interest stops and yours begins.

- Who are your resistors, and which of their objections and arguments are contrary to your plans?
- Do you have a support system that can provide an objective perspective?

## WHERE CAN YOU BE AT YOUR BEST?

➤ **IN HIS BOOK,** *The First 90 Days: Critical Success Strategies for New Leaders at All Levels*, author Michael Watkins makes the point that in order to get off to a strong start in your new job, you must understand your style of working (and leading), and where you can make the most impact. As you approach your new job, use your prior experience as well as your education to confirm where you can be at your best. For example, you may find yourself in a:

# PART I
## GET READY: HOW YOU WORK WITH OTHERS

- Startup venture—where rapid pace and change is the order of the day
- Sustained business—which was built deliberately and runs smoothly most of the time; contributions tend to focus on fine tuning; defense is more important than offense
- Realignment—in which the business is doing okay, but the world is changing—and may be obvious to only a few people; the organization needs people who are perceptive to change and can persuade others when necessary
- Turnaround—high stress, critical need to revamp an existing organization, in which old habits die hard; change can be dramatic and sharp

After earning her MBA, Karen spent two years in a mid-sized company as assistant to the president, a position in which she helped division general managers with capital budgeting and benefits administration. When one of the general managers left the company, the president asked Karen to take that job. Doing so, however, would move her from a sustained business situation at the corporate headquarters to a unit that was in need of a turnaround. As she assessed the opportunity, she became excited about taking on the challenge of a turnaround. But there was still one more issue to consider: would the team support her and help her be successful as she mastered the learning curve for the new assignment?

Karen sought the advice of a neutral third party, a human resources professional who knew her and the team with whom she would be working. The HR person ultimately decided that, yes, Karen would be helped and supported by the team. She accepted the job and was a success.

As Karen's example shows, the more you understand your new environment, the better prepared you will be for the next step of contributing in your new job. The "fit factor" is critical. After all, your new job is meant to be your career launch—not just something you are trying for a couple of years before you move on to something else.

# PART I
## GET READY: HOW YOU WORK WITH OTHERS

- As you review the job description for your new position, what resonates with you—and why?
- Be honest with yourself: Are you taking a job or starting your career?
- What is your next logical career step? How are you preparing for it as you place another tile in your professional mosaic?

## *NOW YOU'RE READY*

**➤ AS YOU GO THROUGH THIS PROCESS OF GETTING READY,** you will engage in self-discovery, identify and confirm strengths and weaknesses, and frame your previous experiences, aptitude, and personality.

At this point, you are ready to make your plan. In the pages that follow, you'll find your "Get Ready" worksheet with spaces for you to identify "Who You Are," "What You Know," and "How You Work with Others."

Then, it's time for the next phase: Get Set!

### *TIPS AND TAKEAWAYS*

➜ Draw on past experiences, no matter how trivial, to help you see where your talents, skills, and aptitudes lie.

➜ Understand the type of assignment that would best suit you and your personality.

➜ Identify your team of supporters, including the family members, friends, and mentors to whom you can turn for advice and feedback.

Your personality and working style will influence the choice of environment in which you feel most comfortable and can contribute the most. When you've found a good match, you will be afforded an opportunity to show leadership on the basis of who you are and what you contribute. ✺

# GET READY.
## PLANNING WORKSHEET

## PERSONAL ON-BOARDING PLAN

|  | 90 DAYS AHEAD<br>**GET READY** | 30 DAYS AHEAD<br>**GET SET** | DAY 1 & FORWARD<br>**GO** |
|---|---|---|---|
| **WHO YOU ARE** | ○ Assess your emotional intelligence<br>○ Understand emotional undercurrents<br>○ Review your experiences<br>○ Use feedback you've received<br>○ Perfect your listening skills | | |
| **WHAT YOU KNOW** | ○ Understand your personality<br>○ Step toward your career dream<br>○ Match position to skills<br>○ Build your experience mosaic | | |
| **HOW YOU WORK WITH OTHERS** | ○ Review previous team experience<br>○ Who's now on your team?<br>○ Beware the resistors<br>○ Where can you be at your best? | | |

# NOTES

## PART II

# GET SET.

**GETTING SET IS ONE OF THE MOST IMPORTANT PROCESSES** for any new hire. It can mean the difference between success in your first job as an MBA and disappointment. This interim step between "Get Ready!" and "Go!" allows you to start at a more informed level and will help propel you to an accelerated trajectory toward greater proficiency in your new job.

There are things you can and should be doing between now and the first day of work that will help you become more effective in your new job, whether your start date is two weeks or several months in the future. Ideally, the "Get Set" phase kicks in within six weeks of your first day on the job. As a *Harvard Business Review* article on the topic suggests, "In the weeks leading up to your new assignment, carve out and hold sacred at least 30 minutes a day to prepare."[3]

In this section, we'll explore the attitudes, aptitudes, and activities that will help you "Get Set," which is an essential interim phase that follows "Get Ready" and precedes "Go!"

"SUCCESSFUL CAREERS ARE NOT PLANNED. THEY DEVELOP WHEN PEOPLE ARE PREPARED FOR OPPORTUNITIES BECAUSE THEY KNOW THEIR STRENGTHS, THEIR METHOD OF WORK AND THEIR VALUES."
—PETER DRUCKER

## PART II
## GET SET

# WHO YOU ARE

**IN TRACK, A RUNNER CAN'T GO DIRECTLY** from get ready to go without stumbling. Getting set transitions the runner from a ready position to being poised to start. It's an interim step, but an essential one that enables the runner to burst out of the starting position with strength and speed.

Similarly, think of a professional golfer who spends hours every day practicing shots. Practicing helps him or her to get ready for the tournament, but even that preparation isn't enough. During the game, the golfer needs to get set before each shot, whether that means envisioning the flight of the ball on a long drive or picturing the roll of the ball across the putting green. Addressing the ball, as it's called, is an important interim step. So it is with you as you start your new job. You've practiced and prepared throughout the interview process, but now it's time to "Get Set."

# PART II
## GET SET: WHO YOU ARE

### *IMAGINING YOUR FIRST DAYS*

➤ **IT'S ESSENTIAL FOR ANY NEW HIRE** to be aware that going from an academic environment to work is a transition. Those who see it as one big continuum usually aren't well-prepared for just how different the environment of their first job will be. Take some time to be reflective, envisioning in your mind what it will be like for you as an MBA on the first day of your new job.

Imagining isn't pretending; it's giving yourself mental images to prepare for what's ahead. The more you can visualize your new company or your new position, the better you will make the transition. In addition, if you have any concerns or questions that you haven't addressed as yet, no doubt they will surface in your visualization.

Steve had his first job lined up to start a month after graduation. Wanting to launch himself successfully, Steve asked me several questions about his first day: How he should dress? How should he act? What could he do to put himself in the most favorable light with his colleagues? Given the questions Steve was asking, I could tell he was 80 percent there. By asking these questions, he demonstrated that he was conscious about the impression he would make from his first day on the job onwards.

Managing initial perceptions is essential. You get one chance here. Psychologists and experts say impressions are made in less than two minutes. Professor Amy Cuddy, a social psychologist, has found that warmth and competence are two critical variables in how people perceive and experience others. As she states, these variables account "for about 80% of our overall evaluations of people (i.e., do you feel good or bad about this person), and shape our emotions and behaviors toward them."[4]

> **MANAGING INITIAL PERCEPTIONS IS ESSENTIAL**

Getting set encompasses the practical as well, from figuring out the

# PART II
## GET SET: WHO YOU ARE

logistics of your commute to honing your people skills. You don't want to leave these plans to the last minute; if you do, you'll find yourself unnecessarily stressed and potentially unprepared. When getting set, ask yourself these key questions:

- How will you get to work? By car? Public transportation? Do you know the route, where you'll park, or what time you have to be at the bus stop or train station? You don't want to be late on your first day.
- If you have to relocate for this new job, do you know the logistics? If you're new to an area, make a couple of practice runs during rush hour to determine the best route and the time it will take you to get to work.
- Do you know some of the specifics of what you will do the first week? Will you have to attend an orientation program for new hires? Did your boss mention, for example, a weekly team meeting on Monday, which you'll attend on your first day?
- Think about the people you met during the interview process, such as coworkers and peers in other departments. Do you remember their names? Do you see yourself spending most of your time with your colleagues, or do you want to expand your network from the beginning to colleagues in other departments?

# PART II

## GET SET: WHO YOU ARE

## *UPDATING YOUR IMAGE*

➤ **YOU'RE NOT A STUDENT ANYMORE.** If the road to getting your MBA took you from work to school and then back to work, you might need to consider your image. You likely need a new wardrobe, or at least an expanded one. You might need a different haircut, even if it's not dramatically different from how you look now. First impressions are critical, not only with your new boss but also with your colleagues. From the first time they meet you, your colleagues will form an impression of what you are like and how it will be to work with you. You can manage that impression by giving some forethought to how you want to be perceived.

Definitely give your image the attention it deserves, but don't obsess over it. Marla, for example, took her mental preparation to the extreme. As the start date of her new job approached, she became increasingly worried about overdressing or underdressing. She asked everyone and anyone for advice on how she should interact with her new coworkers. While preparation is important, overthinking as Marla did will probably result in anxiety, not better preparation. A little information and forethought can go a long way.

# PART II
## GET SET: WHO YOU ARE

- Do you dress like your peers, or are you thinking ahead? Dressing as well as your boss or dressing for your next job are good guidelines when considering how formal your work attire should be.
- Do you know what "business casual" really means? It's definitely not jeans and a t-shirt. Business casual means pressed khakis or other casual pants and a shirt with a collar, but without a tie or jacket.
- Is it time to update your college image for the workforce? Ask a close advisor (as discussed in Part I: Get Ready) for feedback about your appearance, hairstyle, and clothing. There was at one time a smartphone app that allowed you to take your picture and send it to a preselected group of couture experts who critiqued your look.
- Does your body language need a makeover—your posture, your energy level, the impression that you project? For example, some people inadvertently appear to always be in a rush, which could make others think that they are disorganized or can't handle their schedules.

## TIPS AND TAKEAWAYS

→ **Preparing yourself for your job starts with imagining yourself in your new environment.**

→ **Your goal is to make a good impression. You probably don't need an "extreme makeover," but a new look (e.g., shorter hair and more professional attire) may be in the works for you.**

→ **Be conscious about the impression you want to make with your boss, colleagues, and others as you start your new job. You can't rely on your hard work alone; perceptions are reality.**

Getting set is an important interim phase that will prepare you for your exciting new venture. The more reflective you are during this time, the more success you will realize when you start your new job. ✺

PART II

GET SET

# WHAT YOU KNOW

**NOW THAT YOU KNOW THE ORGANIZATION** for which you'll be working, it's time to go deeper. The Internet is your friend as you check out the company's website in more detail, reading press releases and marketing material. Private companies and nonprofits such as museums or foundations will have similar information available. If your new employer is a large, publicly traded company, you will find security analysts' reports, recorded earnings calls with management, product launch press releases, and more about the firm on financial news sites. You might even Google company management to read their bios and speeches that they've given. In addition to published sources, you can also tap personal sources, especially those who are outside the company—such as friends or family members who used to work for the organization. This doesn't have to feel like homework; it should be fun research that gets you excited about your first day on the job.

# PART II

## GET SET: WHAT YOU KNOW

## *EDUCATING YOURSELF TO "GET SET"*

➤ **NOW THAT YOU'VE ACCEPTED THE JOB,** you should know many of the specifics of what you will be doing. (If you don't, you need to find out pretty quickly!) As part of your "Get Set" preparation, explore how what you will be doing fits in with the company's overall mission and purpose. The more you learn about the company and how your position fits into it, the more you will develop a connection that will make your job more meaningful. You will see yourself not just as an employee, but as a contributor of your talents, skills, curiosity, and willingness to learn. When educating yourself about your new company, ask yourself a few key questions:

- How well do you know the company, its businesses, product lines, and services?
- What are the media saying about the company, its business lines, growth prospects, new products, and issues and problems? Set up a Google Alert with your employer, its competitors, and your industry (and related terms) as keywords.
- How can you expand your industry knowledge through related websites, professional organizations, industry groups, and other reputable sources of information?
- Revisit the technical skills that you identified on your resume. Are there gaps between what you said and your true proficiency level in these areas? If so, it's time to address those deficits.

➤ **MAKING THE MOST OF ROTATIONAL ASSIGNMENTS.** The process of getting set applies not only to your first day with the company, but also to the start of each new rotational assignment which will help to make the experience more enjoyable and fulfilling. In the end, you'll be better able to make informed choices about where in the company you could see yourself making the best contribution.

# PART II
## GET SET: WHAT YOU KNOW

At the end of each assignment, ask yourself these questions:
- What are the adjacent business areas that feed information (or goods and materials) to the department in which you'll be working? Develop a broader view rather than a function-specific one.
- How can your particular skills and aptitudes contribute to each department to which you are assigned? Treat each assignment as if you are going to be there permanently, and not just for six or eight weeks.

## KNOWING WHERE YOU CAN MAKE A DIFFERENCE

➤ **SOME GRADUATES, ESPECIALLY** in a challenging job market, will accept a second-choice job, because it's in their first-choice company. For example, a job in sales may be ideal, but a position in customer service is pretty close. If that has happened to you, don't worry. The important thing is you are now with your desired employer. You can always work toward a transfer into your first-choice area. In the meantime, keep an open mind about the job you do have. It could be better than you anticipated.

Matthew had his heart set on working in the marketing department of a particular Fortune 100 consumer products company. He managed to land a job with that organization, but in the research and development department. As he took the R&D position, he told himself, "I'll do a good job where I am and then try to transfer into marketing." To his pleasant surprise, however, his job required him to work closely with the marketing department, becoming a kind of bridge between R&D and marketing. As it turned out, he really liked what he was doing. Bottom line: Give your new job a chance and see what happens. You can make a contribution in any assignment.

As the new hire, you could be taking what looks like a job that no one else wanted. When Kelly accepted a job at a large bank, which was a very prestigious organization, she had a nagging fear about her assignment in the mortgage

# PART II
## GET SET: WHAT YOU KNOW

analysis department. Knowing how problems (such as high-risk, undocumented loans, or loans given to people with lower credit quality) in the bank's mortgage portfolio had contributed to challenges during the recent financial crisis, Kelly was worried. Should she go into such a problem area?

The good news for Kelly is that being assigned to an area in need of change or in the midst of a turnaround is a great way to showcase your ability to make a solid contribution. For one thing, you can't fall off the floor. If the division is already suffering, you'll have far more upside than downside. Anything you can do to help improve things will be noticed right away. Even a small impact could be substantial. Furthermore, a poor-performing division or business unit is probably being watched closely by upper management, which means you may be in the spotlight more than if you started in a healthier division. On the other hand, if the seriousness of the situation is being rationalized and the resistance is deep, be careful that you do not fall in with the negative thinkers.

As you think about how you can make a difference in your new position, consider these factors:

- How can you utilize your analytical skills to understand the specifics and risks involved in your job?
- How does your particular department fit into the overall organization?
- What additional education and training might you need to increase your knowledge and improve your contribution?

# PART II
## GET SET: WHAT YOU KNOW

### TIPS AND TAKEAWAYS

→ **Deepen your knowledge and understanding of your new company and its industry.**

→ **Focus on ways to improve your effectiveness and increase your contribution, right from the start—even if your new position isn't exactly your dream job.**

Educate yourself about your employer and the requirements of your new job. Rather than view this interim phase as homework, see it as an investment in your own success.

PART II

GET SET

# HOW YOU WORK WITH OTHERS

**A**S YOU GET SET, IT'S NORMAL TO FOCUS MOSTLY ON YOURSELF. After all, you're the one who is taking a new job. In the context of your preparation, however, you should also give thought to the people with whom you will be working. As a fresh MBA with extensive prior experience, you may be assigned to lead your own team. Your relationship with colleagues at all levels of the organization will have a significant influence on how you work and how successful you'll be at your job.

No matter what your specific job will be, with every assignment you may become part of an entirely new team. Envisioning the team and how you will contribute to it from the start is a big part of "getting set" in your new job.

# PART II
## GET SET: HOW YOU WORK WITH OTHERS

# COMMUNICATION STYLE: IT'S ALL ABOUT YOUR BOSS

▶ **BRIAN HAD BEEN ON THE JOB ONLY A FEW DAYS.** While he was on the phone, his boss leaned in his cubicle and mouthed, "See me when you have a moment." When Brian ended the phone call, he sent his boss a quick email with the subject line "What's up?"

From this short interaction it's clear that Brian has a lot to learn about making his style of working fit with the company culture. As the new person, you will be expected to adapt to the manager's work style—not the other way around. You may be used to instant messaging and texting, but your boss may prefer face-to-face communication. In that case, your boss's style wins.

Another aspect of communication is how accessible and responsive people are outside of work hours. Is 24/7 communication the norm? Do your boss and colleagues send emails at night and on the weekend? Also, what is the format for communication? Is it formal and structured prose? Is a quick note with bullet points acceptable? (Beware the smiley face sign-off if you're the only one using it.)

Communication reflects corporate culture. Companies (and industries) have personalities all their own, which may reflect the preferences of top management that are emulated by managers and teams all the way down the line. In addition, some divisions have subcultures that may depart from or have a different flavor than the overall corporate culture. The third layer is your boss's style, tone, and personality. The better you understand the culture and subcultures going in, the more easily you will adapt. As you look ahead to your new position, keep in mind some important issues when it comes to communicating with the members of your new group:

# PART II
## GET SET: HOW YOU WORK WITH OTHERS

- Avoid all text-speak (BTW, FYEO, THX, LOL, etc.) in your emails and memos. If your boss is fond of using it, you can adapt, but don't overdo it. You need to demonstrate your corporate communication maturity and professionalism.
- Does your company tend to have a lot of short meetings in which everything is laid on the table in a free-form discussion? Or, does it have fewer formal meetings with long, written documents that are prepared by departments and individual contributors?

The more you know about the organization's communication style and expectations, the better and more quickly you will fit in.

## HAVE A GET SET CONVERSATION

➤ **YOUR MANAGER IS THE GATEWAY** to getting you on an extraordinary onboarding trajectory. He or she will lead you to meeting the right people, provide suggested readings, help identify a broader affinity group, and, in gen-

# PART II
## GET SET: HOW YOU WORK WITH OTHERS

eral, make your arrival smooth. You won't be expected to know everything on your first day at work, but there are important insights you can glean ahead of time to get a head start. One way to gain these insights is by talking to your boss before you start your job.

Approach your boss about a month before your start date, requesting a meeting or a phone conversation to address a few of your questions and to find out what he or she would like you to know and to read ahead of time. If your boss prefers to answer your questions via email, that's fine—and it tells you something about his or her communication style. Whatever form your conversation takes, having a "Get Set" discussion will improve your understanding while demonstrating your commitment to your boss. Some questions to pose include:

- What additional information should you have before you start your job in order to be better prepared on the first day?
- What rules, regulations, and protocols should you be aware of before you start? One area to investigate thoroughly is approval levels. As the new hire, to whom will you go to get permission or approval?
- Who on the team should you meet first? As you converse with your boss, you may get tips or suggestions about your colleagues and how best to get to know them.
- Who are the other people who will be crucial to your onboarding success? These people may not be on your team, so you need to keep your eyes open in order to interact with them as soon as possible.
- What additional reading would your boss recommend to further your preparation?
- Would your boss like to see your personal onboarding plan? If so, you may decide to share only the most relevant portions of it.

# PART II
## GET SET: HOW YOU WORK WITH OTHERS

## DEVELOP A TEAM MINDSET

▶ **AS THE NEW MBA ON THE TEAM,** you certainly hope to be welcomed by your new colleagues (although that is not always the case, as you recall from the "resisters" discussed in Part I: Get Ready). As you get set for that first day, however, you will want to make sure you have a team mindset. Your focus should be as much on your colleagues and being a member of a team as it is on yourself.

Self-awareness is crucial. As you rehearse in your mind your first day on the job, think about your interactions with your colleagues. You certainly don't want to script every conversation, but you do want to develop greater awareness to avoid pitfalls of unintended behavior.

When Greg was offered a job transfer to Little Rock, he made it clear to management that he didn't want to spend more than two or three years in that assignment. He had recently married, and he and his wife were both from Connecticut, where they wanted to settle down and eventually raise a family. Those longer-term personal plans for relocating, however, could not color his interaction with his colleagues and direct reports. Wanting to show his commitment to the job (and his new community) in a very tangible way, Greg and his wife bought a townhouse in Little Rock instead of renting. No matter that his plan was to be transferred back to Connecticut in twenty-four to thirty-six months; he needed to visualize the Little Rock assignment as permanent and act like it—internally and externally.

As you think about how you can connect with your team, consider these questions:

- As you evaluate your boss's comments and suggestions in your initial "Get Set" conversation, what strategies and outreach will you use with your colleagues? (Note: In some progressive companies, you could be assigned a mentor. If so, then you should reach out to that person in advance of your start date.)

# PART II
## GET SET: HOW YOU WORK WITH OTHERS

- Who are the people with whom you will be working most closely? Get to know their roles and responsibilities.
- How are you thinking about your new job? As a great opportunity for your present and your future? Or as a temporary assignment before you go on to what (and where) you really want?

# PART II
## GET SET: HOW YOU WORK WITH OTHERS

### TIPS AND TAKEAWAYS

→ Utilize the results of your "Get Set" conversation with your new boss to better your chances of having an exceptional transition.

→ Develop the mindset of a team player, even before you start your new job.

→ Get to know all you can about the company, the department, your manager, and the team with whom you'll be working.

Getting set may seem like a lot of work (and it is!), especially if you're busy with finals and graduation, or if you were hoping to take some time for rest and relaxation before starting your new job. The process, however, should be fun and engaging.

The more committed you are to making good use of the interim between job acceptance and start date, the better chance you'll have to launch your career in a positive way. As you prepare, visualize what's in store for you, from your daily commute to your daily tasks. Once you're set, then it will be time to "Go!" ☀

# NOTES

# GET SET.
## PLANNING WORKSHEET

## PERSONAL ON-BOARDING PLAN

|  | 90 DAYS AHEAD<br>**GET READY** | 30 DAYS AHEAD<br>**GET SET** | DAY 1 & FORWARD<br>**GO** |
|---|---|---|---|
| **WHO YOU ARE** | ○ Assess your emotional intelligence<br>○ Understand emotional undercurrents<br>○ Review your experiences<br>○ Use feedback you've received<br>○ Perfect your listening skills | ○ Visualize "Getting Set"<br>○ Imagine your first days<br>○ Confirm the logistics<br>○ Update your image<br>○ Act consistent with your role<br>○ Plan to manage impressions |  |
| **WHAT YOU KNOW** | ○ Understand your personality<br>○ Step toward your career dream<br>○ Match position to skills<br>○ Build your experience mosaic | ○ Educate yourself to "Get Set"<br>○ Find indirect company contacts<br>○ Set-up Google alerts<br>○ Make a difference<br>○ Fill in skill gaps |  |
| **HOW YOU WORK WITH OTHERS** | ○ Review previous team experience<br>○ Who's now on your team?<br>○ Beware the resistors<br>○ Where can you be at your best? | ○ Use boss's communication style<br>○ Have a get-set conversation<br>○ Get reading recommendations<br>○ Learn about job expectations, rules, culture, issues, etc.<br>○ Identify extended team<br>○ Develop a team mind-set |  |

# "SUCCESS IS DEPENDENT ON EFFORT."
—SOPHOCLES

## PART III

# GO!

**YOUR FIRST DAY ON THE JOB HAS ARRIVED.** Thanks to all your hard work getting ready and getting set, you are well prepared. Now you can go! Your focus should always be on how you add value to the organization, given your background, expertise, and the job you've been given.

The preparation work you've done already will begin to pay off immediately. You are starting off on the extraordinary onboarding trajectory. The head start you've gained will yield dividends from the moment you walk in the office, increasing your confidence and your contribution.

As a new MBA, you may be the junior person on the team, or you might be a manager. Even though you may be low in the organizational hierarchy, don't underestimate the positive impact you can have on your teammates. And

# PART III
## GO

remember, no job or task is beneath you. If someone asks you to do something seemingly trivial or even menial—for example, taking a package to the mailroom or picking up supplies—do what's expected and do it with a smile. You may have been in the top 5 percent of your MBA cohort, but on the job you're the new person. Find ways to distinguish yourself by volunteering to do the jobs no one else wants to do. It's not about you anymore; it's all about the team.

Understand, too, that you may have some negative perceptions to counter. A study by Workplace Options found that 77 percent of workers believe that Millennials have a different attitude toward workplace responsibilities compared with other age groups; 68 percent think that Millennials are less motivated to take on responsibilities and produce quality work; and 46 percent are of the opinion that Millennials are less engaged at work than others. In addition, of the Millennials who were surveyed, 55 percent said they believed peers in their own age group were less motivated to take on job responsibilities, and 34 percent said their peers were less engaged than their more mature counterparts.[5]

Understanding what you're up against will help you manage how others view your level of engagement and motivation. If you can show that you are the exception to what is perceived to be the rule, you will distinguish yourself as you optimize the opportunity you've been given. ✸

## PART III

### GO

# WHO YOU ARE

**YOU ARE YOUR BEST ASSET.** Beyond where you went to school, your degree, your previous experience, and everything that makes up your resume, you are what you bring to work every day. If you arrive the first day with a great attitude and genuine enthusiasm, you will increase your chance of success immeasurably. However, if in the back of your mind your attitude is "I'm just going to pass through here in order to get my ticket punched until I go on to the next thing," then you can't fake it. People will notice. You have to be sincere in your desire to fit in and make a contribution.

# PART III
## GO: WHO YOU ARE

## IT STARTS WITH A SMILE

▶ **MAKING A POSITIVE FIRST IMPRESSION** happens in the first few seconds. You have visualized this; now do it! The moment you meet your colleagues on your first day, greet them warmly and sincerely. Go in with a smile as you introduce yourself. Have a grateful attitude and a "thank you" for everyone who helps you (which, given that you're new, will happen all day long). It may seem like a small gesture, but it can pay off big.

Alicia is a friendly person by nature; she is warm and outgoing. When she started her new job, it was second nature for her to be cheerful and smiley and always appreciative of others. After a year, she had a performance appraisal. Her boss was complimentary of her work, and she received a better-than-average raise in pay. "You've done a fantastic job," her boss explained. "Not only is your work excellent, but you're always smiling. We never have to worry about motivating you because you're so positive and upbeat."

When Alicia told me this story, she was convinced that having a smile every day helped her to become more successful in her new job and to be recognized in a positive way.

As you begin your new job, think about the impression you're making on your new colleagues:

- How do others perceive you? Do you treat everyone with the same respect? Do you come across as friendly and cheerful, or do you tend to be more withdrawn and aloof? You don't have to adopt a new personality, but having a pleasant attitude toward others will elevate the impression you make.
- Is saying "thank you" a habit? If it does not come naturally to you, then be conscious and deliberate about acknowledging others. Your gratitude will encourage people to help you even more.
- Do you make it a point to remember names? When someone tells you his or her name, repeat it aloud: "It's a pleasure to meet you, John."

# PART III

## GO: WHO YOU ARE

Make a mental note of what John looks like (e.g., tall guy with glasses and dark hair) and write it down if it helps you. When you end a conversation, repeat the person's name. "Thanks again, John. I appreciate your help." If you say the name a few times, you are more apt to remember it.

- Do you feel confident shaking hands? Image and personal branding expert Roz Usheroff advises people to shake hands long enough to notice the person's eye color. Both men and women should shake hands with the same grip, strength, and duration.

## THE NETWORK BEYOND YOUR CUBICLE

▶ **CECELIA WAS ON THE JOB FOR ONLY NINE MONTHS** when she was encouraged by her boss to apply for a job in a different department. When Cecelia asked why she was being considered for this opportunity, her boss explained that another department head had been impressed with the work she did on a cross-functional team. When a job opened up in that department, the leader approached Cecelia's current boss to ask if she would apply.

As this example shows, the impression you make can extend far beyond your cubicle. The quality of your work, your

# PART III

## GO: WHO YOU ARE

willingness and eagerness to pitch in, and your positive attitude will attract others who may very well open the door to the next opportunity for you. It all starts with an attitude of openness to new opportunities and people beyond your team.

From your first day on the job, you will become part of formal and informal affinity groups that will include, for example, peers and colleagues in your department, people with whom you interact in other departments, and even those with whom you share personal interests, such as volunteering for a company charity endeavor or a physical fitness event. Your company may also sponsor employee networking groups comprised of segments of the employee population, such as groups based on ethnicity or on common interests or concerns. Attending brown bag lunches will also broaden your network and demonstrate your commitment.

Over time, your affinity groups will morph and be refined. If the group you are looking for does not exist, then create it! Find those whose perspectives enhance your learning and experiences. Ask yourself who might be able to help keep you on the right path.

One word of caution: As the new person, you may find that the people in your department or on your team want to befriend you. Although it's great to have warm and collegial relationships with your peers and coworkers, be careful not to be confined to one group of people.

It's also possible that you may be seen as a high-potential employee and your boss expects you to be a strong performer, which makes people want to befriend you.

# PART III

## GO: WHO YOU ARE

Don't limit your circle to the same people who want to go out for coffee or to lunch every day with you. Establish a wide base of friendships. (In fact, you don't have to find your best friends at work—especially if you live in an urban area. In a smaller geographic area, most people you meet may work for the same company. If so, be sure to maintain professionalism in your relationships.) Although you may be paired with certain people on assignments, look for opportunities to reach out beyond your team. Asking others for advice is an excellent way to build new relationships in different departments. These are tangible ways for you to make the most of your networking on the job and expand your circle of contacts into a rich mosaic of interests, talents, and perspectives.

Former classmates, particularly those with varied backgrounds, are another way to network with a broader variety of people. As you meet with these contacts, you'll get out of your own environment and expand your horizons. It's always a good idea to develop an informal network of people who have far different backgrounds than yours, such as lawyers, accountants, consultants, artists, musicians, or even members of the clergy. As they introduce you to their contacts, you will find your network-building has become contagious!

- As you expand your professional network, think about how to make it as broad and diverse as possible: in what ways have you consciously expanded your professional network outside your team or department?
- How willing are you to share your expertise freely with others? Helping others allows you to build your informal network and practice your servant leadership—putting others first and demonstrating your willingness to share.
- How open are you to meeting and working with others, even if that means volunteering for a task force or project that involves extra work?
- Do you choose assignments based on what you will learn, or are you only interested in the "glitz" of a choice assignment where you will be recognized or rub shoulders with senior managers?
- Do you know the "connectors" in the workplace who can facilitate

# PART III

## GO: WHO YOU ARE

key introductions? Often, administrative assistants, especially on the executive level, are the gatekeepers and people in the know who can help make things happen for you.

## BE RESILIENT

➤ **AS YOU FOCUS ON THE POSITIVE,** keep in mind that no job is perfect. Chances are that within the first month you will encounter something negative. Perhaps it's a situation that didn't go your way. Or you may be disappointed because your new employer is not able to deliver on everything that had been promised. The job that you were so excited about may seem boring and routine at times.

Don't be a whiner! Every position, especially those early on in your career, provides valuable lessons and experiences. Look beyond slights and temporary setbacks and view the total opportunity that you've been given. Try to take the company's point of view and consider the possibility that your perception may be distorted or too short-term. It's possible that doing "X" right now, which is not your first choice, may be more important than being engaged in "Y," which you'd prefer to be doing. As you look at the overall assignment and all its challenges and learning experiences, you will probably see that the good outweighs the bad.

- Is the disappointment you're facing a deal-breaker on the job—or just a temporary setback? Talking with your trusted advisor may help you get a better perspective.
- How can you adjust your own attitude and expectations to improve the situation?

# PART III

## GO: WHO YOU ARE

### TIPS AND TAKEAWAYS

→ Know that success starts with your attitude. Your eagerness, enthusiasm, humble confidence, and genuine desire to contribute to the team will support a positive first impression.

→ Keep your perspective around disappointments and setbacks. No job is perfect. The roadblock you face today could very well be temporary.

→ Say "please" and "thank you." It may sound simple and obvious, but you'd be surprised how well it works (and how many people consistently fail to show graciousness and gratitude consistently).

→ Continuously build your network inside and outside the company to broaden your horizons and deepen your perspective.

Focus on the "golden rule" of the workplace: Treat others the way you would have them treat you. Show respect, willingness to help, and gratitude. Your success depends on it. ✺

# PART III
## GO: WHO YOU ARE

**A NEW EMPLOYEE IN THE SHIPPING DEPARTMENT CAREFULLY TIES BOWS ON EVERY PACKAGE, TAKING PRIDE IN THIS ADDED TOUCH. HIS SUPERVISOR STOPS BY HIS WORKSTATION TO ASK WHY HE'S DOING THIS.**

**"IN MY LAST JOB, CUSTOMERS RAVED ABOUT THE WAY I DECORATED THEIR PACKAGES," THE EMPLOYEE EXPLAINS.**

**"TELL ME AGAIN WHERE YOUR LAST JOB WAS," THE BOSS CONTINUES.**

**"SMITH'S GIFTS AND FINE CHINA— IN THE CUSTOMER CARE DEPARTMENT."**

**THE BOSS NODS. "AH, THAT EXPLAINS IT. BUT YOU DO KNOW WE SELL INDUSTRIAL PARTS, RIGHT?"**

PART III

GO

# WHAT YOU KNOW

**YOU BRING TO YOUR NEW ROLE THE KNOWLEDGE** that you've gained elsewhere, whether from classes or from previous jobs that you've had. Some of your technical skills—such as making an Excel spreadsheet or collecting receivables—may be directly applicable in your new job, but every work environment is different. You may, for example, have experience dealing with consumers, but the company sells to industrial end users, which affects the terms and conditions as well as the practices of your job. Observe how your colleagues perform their tasks. Learn from them.

# PART III
## GO: WHAT YOU KNOW

As you dig into your first assignments, you will run into things you don't know how to do—even as an MBA. If so, don't try to hide it. No one will expect you to know how to do everything or understand the nuances of how things are done for your new employer. Beware the desire to impress others, especially your boss. Identify the "teachers" around you, especially those from cross functions who have coached your peers. Reach out to them for help and advice.

The first project you undertake will solidify others' impression of you. In a word, it must be excellent (no typos, grammatical mistakes, or simple math errors). On the other hand, don't gloss over what you don't know. Ask for advice, clarification, feedback, and guidance. Most people, you'll find, are more than willing to help, especially if you have a genuinely humble and grateful attitude.

As a new hire, you need to find the courage to speak up when you see something that doesn't make sense or when you have a suggestion. You don't have to be a know-it-all; nor should you act arrogant in any way. You can be gentle and sincere as you ask others to explain how things work and what might be improved.

My first job out of Harvard Business School was with clothing manufacturer Hart Schaffner & Marx. As a new employee, I encountered the problem that custom-made suits were consistently shipped behind schedule. As I tried to find the reason, I asked everyone involved in the process. Since I was the new guy, it was only natural that I would ask in-depth questions about how things worked. When I politely inquired, the seamstresses and tailors were more than willing to explain the situation: the way they were compensated made it more advantageous to work on standardized items rather than custom-made suits. Once I understood the problem, I could help devise a solution.

You can do the same in your new position. Ask questions. Seek insight from your colleagues. Your goal is to broaden the scope of your understanding.

- Do you assume you know everything about performing a certain task? Although your knowledge and previous experiences are valuable,

# PART III

## GO: WHAT YOU KNOW

be sure you know how well they translate to your new assignment.
- Do you boast about your big-name school at every opportunity? If so, don't. Let people get to know you first. Then, when they discover your background, they'll be impressed. If you wear it on your sleeve, it could turn people off.
- Do you talk about how the training at your school excelled in a particular area, or how you mastered a particular task in your last job? Don't qualify what you know. Just do your work and let your results speak for themselves.
- Are you able to recognize the gaps in your knowledge? Deepen your understanding by talking with others, doing research, and reading. As one former student told me, the first six months on the job felt like "constantly cramming for exams, day after day." Recognize that's what it takes. These demands are not going to change, particularly in assignments such as consulting.
- Do you easily admit to what you don't know? Faking it won't help anyone—especially you. Ask questions early; it's expected. If you wait too long, people will wonder if you haven't been paying attention or if you lack the confidence to speak up.
- How do you determine the value of your work? Its true worth is how well your input (data, a report, spreadsheet, etc.) can be used by others.
- Are you thinking ahead to your next assignment as your proficiency builds? You can have a plan without being too ambitious or spending an inordinate amount of time thinking about your next job so that you neglect your current one.

# PART III
## GO: WHAT YOU KNOW

### TIPS AND TAKEAWAYS

→ **Look for ways to apply your knowledge and skills as you take on your first assignments, but never assume you have all the answers.**

→ **Ask questions, seek guidance, and do research to bridge your knowledge gaps with new understanding.**

→ **Request more training and experience, such as on cross-functional teams and special assignments.**

What you know helped you to land your job, but your willingness to expand your knowledge and deepen your understanding as you work with others will determine your success.

# NOTES

## PART III
## GO

# HOW YOU WORK WITH OTHERS

**Y**ou've been given your first assignment. Now it's time to show what you can do. The first rule: underpromise and overdeliver. Never sacrifice quality for speed. For example, if you promise that you will deliver a project by May 25, privately commit yourself to an earlier deadline, such as May 15—provided that you produce high-quality work. If you need the extra ten days to deliver, you won't break your commitment.

Look for ways to establish an early win, such as completing a task or project that is important to your boss or that is needed by other people in the organization. However, you have to be discerning where early wins are concerned. They must involve your team, be relatively low cost, and be perceived by others as valuable. How you work and the results you produce speak volumes about you.

# PART III

## GO: HOW YOU WORK WITH OTHERS

## MANAGING YOUR BOSS

➤ **YOUR TOP PRIORITY IN YOUR NEW** job is to manage your boss. This means making sure that what you are doing supports your boss's priorities. Don't focus on something extraneous to your assignment because you think it's interesting or fun; make sure that your efforts align with what your boss thinks is most important.

To forge a connection with your boss, you'll need to follow his or her communication style; for example, find out whether he or she wants to have short in-person conversations or prefers updates by email. Know how frequently your boss wants to be updated on your progress. It's better to overcommunicate with updates (at least weekly) and then scale back than it is to have your boss say, "You need to let me know what you're doing."

## PART III
### GO: HOW YOU WORK WITH OTHERS

No matter how your boss likes to communicate, make sure he or she is informed. One of the biggest frustrations for managers is when they don't know something. When it doubt, inform! As a cautionary tale, consider Adam, who thought his newly minted MBA was license to do things his way. Adam repeatedly ignored his boss's request that he provide details about his business travel plans and contact list. Instead, he set his own priorities for the customers he wanted to see and the accounts he thought were most important. When his boss asked him about the missing information, Adam defended his tactics by saying he was a self-starter. His performance was erratic and not consistently excellent.

Ultimately, Adam's maverick reputation spread among his boss's colleagues, who did not support his behavior, and he was blocked from future promotions. After less than a year, Adam left the company. In retrospect, some of Adam's initiatives were effective and produced desirable results. Had he communicated proactively and forged a stronger relationship with his boss, Adam may have found the support he needed to be successful.

When you think about ways to establish rapport with your boss, consider these issues:

- Do you know your boss's agenda? Make sure everything you do supports his or her priorities.
- Do you update your boss frequently enough, or are you receiving emails and voicemails asking you to report on your progress? Are you timely in your responses? When in doubt, overcommunicate.
- Have you established a strong relationship with your boss's administrative assistant? As noted previously, he or she acts as a facilitator, so gaining his or her confidence and support is invaluable.

# PART III
## GO: HOW YOU WORK WITH OTHERS

## TAKING ON MORE WORK— ESPECIALLY JOBS NO ONE ELSE WANTS

> *As King Arthur held court with his Knights of the Round Table, he looked for a volunteer to help around the royal stables. No one spoke up. Sir Lindsey of Limelight kept his eyes on his reflection in his shiny armor. Sir Egbert of Headstrong gazed upward as if pondering deep thoughts. Finally, one of the pages spoke up, "I'll help you, Sire." And so the least of the lot got King Arthur's attention by his willingness to pitch in and do the royal dirty work. When it came time for the annual review of pages, and to see who might be moved to the knight-in-training track, guess who was at the top of the list? Moral of the story: When the boss looks for volunteers for a task you can do (or are willing to learn), speak up!*

▶ **DOING THE JOBS THAT NO ONE WANTS** (reorganizing the supply closet, inputting numbers in that monster database...) is an excellent way to showcase your work ethic, desire to contribute, and your focus on the team. Your boss will be pleased, although there could be some colleagues who resent your efforts and see them as political and a way to ingratiate yourself—so beware.

Jack had been on the job two weeks when his boss announced at a staff meeting that the filing had backed up and needed to be tackled. When no one volunteered, Jack agreed to do it. People noticed. His boss was pleased at his willingness to take on such an unwanted job. A few of his colleagues were impressed by his positive attitude and offered to help him. As for those who grumbled and rolled their eyes, Jack chose to ignore them.

# PART III
## GO: HOW YOU WORK WITH OTHERS

After you've been on the job longer, you may learn of other opportunities to expand your contribution. For example, there may be cross-department taskforces. When your boss asks for a volunteer, offer your assistance (that is, provided you have enough time and mental bandwidth for the project without sacrificing your regular responsibilities). In a more informal capacity, if you notice that one of your colleagues needs help, particularly in an area in which you have some proficiency (for example, in Excel), then offer to help.

Taking on more tasks can be a good way to demonstrate your enthusiasm and proficiency. But be sure not to overcommit and spread yourself too thin. As you think about ways to expand your horizons, consider these questions:

- How willing are you to volunteer to do the dirty work? Do you think that certain tasks are beneath you?
- Do you have a tendency to take on too much? Multitasking makes you less productive, not more.
- Do you try to deliver more than is expected, without going to an extreme? Set a reasonable pace for overdelivering, without raising the bar excessively (e.g., completing a two-week project in three days). You will not be able to maintain that pace, and there could be some holes in your work.
- How good are you at noticing obvious errors you've made? Becoming a better proofreader and estimator should be part of your regular routine and is even more important when you're taking on extra tasks that could make you feel more pressure. Read what you've written aloud to yourself, which will help you find typos and dropped words. Use estimating to discover mathematical errors in your work before someone else does. (e.g., if you say something is a 100 percent increase or a 50 percent decrease, does that make sense?)
- Are you open to assignments outside your department? These may not be choice jobs or glamorous assignments, but opportunities to get to know others in the organization will increase your knowledge and your exposure.

# PART III

## GO: HOW YOU WORK WITH OTHERS

## DON'T GET DISTRACTED

➤ **IT'S NORMAL TO LIKE SOME PARTS OF YOUR JOB** better than others. For example, you may love doing research but dislike writing reports. Every job at every level—including when you're the boss one day—will have its pluses and minuses. Don't get distracted by your personal preferences. Remember, you want to focus on your boss's agenda.

This discipline will serve you well later on when you're the team leader or manager. If you push your own personal agenda—the pet projects that you think are the most important—you'll undermine your contribution because you won't be focused on the company's (and your boss's) priorities. (Certain companies like Google and 3M allow you to spend time on what you want to work on, but they are the exceptions.)

Another big distraction for new employees is the social side of work: the company softball team, after work get-togethers, and so forth. If you focus too much on being a social butterfly instead of on getting your work done, you'll soon find that your wings have been clipped. As you keep your eye on the bottom line—fulfilling your boss's mission—consider ways to keep from becoming distracted.

- Are you focused on your work—or on the social side of working? Word to the wise: don't date anyone at work.
- What do you spend most of your time and effort on? Make sure you remain on track with your boss's agenda.

## GETTING USED TO THE QUIRKS

After spending two months on the job, Charlie had a conversation with his trusted advisor, who wanted to know how things were going. "You won't believe how messed up this place is!" Charlie exclaimed. "The managers can't make a decision. It takes forever to get anything done. And half the people seem to be doing things that are completely unnecessary!"

# PART III
## GO: HOW YOU WORK WITH OTHERS

"Really?" his advisor replied. "Do you suppose that it's possible you don't have a full understanding of how things work yet? Keep your eyes and your mind open. Observe without judging and see if you change your mind."

Two months later, Charlie met his trusted advisor for lunch. "You were right," he said sheepishly. "I understand now why things are done this way. The company operates in a pretty tough regulatory environment, so there are lots of checks and balances. I do think there are some things that I can do more efficiently in my own job, but I'm going to wait to talk to my boss after I know more of the facts."

As Charlie discovered, every place has its quirks—the quixotic habits and puzzling ways of doing things. Certain procedures may seem unnecessary or outdated. Some individuals on the team may appear to be getting special treatment. When you're the new employee, it's difficult to see the subtleties behind the scenes. What appears on the surface to be an indirect or inefficient method may, in fact, be a pretty good work-around.

On the flip side, there may be some things that need to be changed or that are simply nonsense. As discussed earlier, over time and with input from your boss, you'll be able to identify those things that can be changed in order to make the process smoother and more efficient.

As you settle in your new position and begin to recognize the idiosyncrasies of the organization, ask yourself these questions (before you become too frustrated with perceived ineptitudes!):

- Which sensitive areas related to your new job do everyone accept without question? These may be the quirky things you discover about procedures that make no sense at first, but which usually have a ratio-

# PART III
## GO: HOW YOU WORK WITH OTHERS

nale behind them.

• Who is treated like the exception to the rule? This may be the person who comes in later than everyone else or a high performer who doesn't appear to follow the norms. Know that there may be very good reasons for these arrangements, which do not apply to you.

• Do you not fit in? Frequently the problem is getting along with your boss (see "'Managing' Your Boss.") If so, try to find a way to work together. If the issue is the value system of the organization, that will not change. You will either have to change your values (and be careful of that one!), or you will have to leave.

## GROUP DYNAMICS

▶ **WHEN YOU GO TO A TEAM MEETING,** who gets listened to and who is shut out? What happens when people voice an opinion or offer an idea? What gets follow-up and what is ignored and shot down? These are some of the nuances of the workplace that you, as the new person, need to observe. The more aware you become of the group dynamics from the start, the better able you'll be to navigate the playing field—and the players.

As the new person, when is it acceptable for you to speak up in team meetings? The answer depends a lot on your personality, your team dynamics, and what you're working on. In the beginning, you'll undoubtedly do more listening than talking, but fairly quickly you'll be invited into the discussion. As you feel more comfortable and have something substantive to contribute, you should feel free to join the discourse. Understanding group dynamics help you tailor your comments and engagement.

# PART III
## GO: HOW YOU WORK WITH OTHERS

- How do people react to each other and to you? Brush up on your emotional intelligence skills. Observe people's nonverbal communications—their reactions and decisions in response to others.
- How are decisions made? Does the process appear to be fast, or is it slowed by continual requests for more information?
- Do certain people dominate the team meetings while others remain quiet? What happens when someone speaks up to ask a question or request more information?

## *WHO KNOWS WHO KNOWS WHOM?*

▶ **IN EVERY COMPANY, THERE ARE PEOPLE WHO ARE IN THE KNOW.** These are the folks who know how things work and why. These people may not have the most impressive titles, and they may not even be in your department. But these individuals, either through longevity or the relationships that they've built, understand the inner workings and the personalities within the organization. Equally important, they know who knows whom—and who knows what! If you are open-minded and show respect, those in the know will find you and help you out. Now is the time to be sure you're tapping into your affinity group and the list of contacts your boss provided. Beware: use your affinity group for information, not gossip.

The concept of using your contacts to make new connections mirrors the new wave of social networking (e.g., LinkedIn). The more sophisticated companies are using social networking and intranets for assembling teams and building rapport. Some even use it for market intelligence and data analytics. Keep your networking skills up to date.

As you make your way in your new job, keep an eye on who knows what and who knows whom. Look for ways to build that network.

# PART III
## GO: HOW YOU WORK WITH OTHERS

- Who are the go-to people for answers? Introduce yourself and show respect in your interactions. These are the people you need on your side.
- How can you use your people skills and your social networking to get to know those who know?

## ETHICAL DILEMMAS

➤ **EVERY YEAR, I TALK TO STUDENTS** at Northwestern University about a topic that many of them hope they'll never encounter in their careers: ethical dilemmas. The truth is that ethical situations arise sooner than you think and may be more common than you realize.

For example, in 2007, a year before the financial crisis hit, James took a job as a manager with a mortgage originator. After a month or so on the job, he noticed that the credit quality of loans being approved seemed very low. On several occasions, James felt pressure from his boss for his team to approve loans that he felt should be rejected. He discussed the situation with his trusted advisor, who agreed there seemed to be a problem with the company's business practices. His advisor encouraged James to talk to his boss. When James asked his boss about the loan approvals, he was told, "That's how we do things here. Our job is to originate the loans. Whether or not the borrowers can pay is someone else's problem." James immediately began looking for another job.

As the new hire in the company, you need to be aware of ethical issues. If a certain practice appears questionable, there may be a perfectly legitimate reason for it. If you have nagging doubts, go to your trusted advisor for an outside opinion. If there is an issue, then go to your boss. Never compromise your ethics.

- Is there anything in your company's work practices that causes you concern?
- How comfortable do you feel going to your boss to discuss the situation?

# PART III
## GO: HOW YOU WORK WITH OTHERS

- If your boss's actions are the problem, can you go to a trusted advisor inside the company, to HR, or to your boss's boss?
- Have your colleagues ever expressed the same reservations that you are now feeling?

## LOOK FOR MENTORS

➤ **BE ON THE LOOKOUT FOR POSSIBLE NEW MENTORS** who are willing to invest in the next phase of your development. You may meet your mentor through a particular assignment, such as when you reach out to others in a different department for advice, guidance, or to work cross-functionally. This mentor, particularly one outside your department, may see in you a promising person who deserves an investment of time and effort. In addition, you can be more proactive by asking someone you respect for advice, following it, and evaluating the result; if favorable, ask for more. Before you know it, a mentoring relationship is established.

A mentor who has been with the organization for several years can teach you important lessons, such as how more senior people do their jobs, how decisions are made in the company, and how involved leaders are with others in the organization. This is invaluable insight into the corporate culture that you can gain early on through a mentor.

Building a mentor relationship can help you in your new job—and throughout your career. As you seek to build that relationship, consider these important issues:

- Do you remember to say thank you and report your progress after you've taken your mentor's advice? If you never close this loop, you may find your mentor is unwilling to help you in the future.
- Are you making yourself available to others especially as you network with people in other departments?

# PART III

## GO: HOW YOU WORK WITH OTHERS

- Are you sensitive to people who may be trying to mentor or coach you?
- Are your ears open to the subtle hints and suggestions that people are giving about new opportunities and chances to learn?

## TIPS AND TAKEAWAYS

→ **Your first boss wields an undeniable influence on your job performance —and your career. Make sure you are working for someone you like and whose values you admire.**

→ **Your job comes down to one thing: making your boss happy and the team look good. Don't lose sight of this simple fact.**

How you work and the results you achieve are the final proof of whether your boss has made a good decision in hiring you.

After devoting time and effort to "Getting Ready", and "Getting Set," you can "Go" with confidence and enthusiasm. Your first job will set the tone for your success in the years ahead. By keeping your focus on the team and making your boss's agenda your top priority, you will launch yourself brilliantly into your new career.

# NOTES

# GO! PLANNING WORKSHEET

## PERSONAL ON-BOARDING PLAN

| | 90 DAYS AHEAD<br>**GET READY** | 30 DAYS AHEAD<br>**GET SET** | DAY 1 & FORWARD<br>**GO** |
|---|---|---|---|
| **WHO YOU ARE** | ○ Assess your emotional intelligence<br>○ Understand emotional undercurrents<br>○ Review your experiences<br>○ Use feedback you've received<br>○ Perfect your listening skills | ○ Visualize "Getting Set"<br>○ Imagine your first days<br>○ Confirm the logistics<br>○ Update your image<br>○ Act consistent with your role<br>○ Plan to manage impressions | ○ Start with the right attitude, a smile, please and thank you<br>○ Appear warm and approachable<br>○ Treat everyone the same<br>○ Remember names<br>○ Network beyond your cubicle<br>○ Be resilient |
| **WHAT YOU KNOW** | ○ Understand your personality<br>○ Step toward your career dream<br>○ Match position to skills<br>○ Build your experience mosaic | ○ Educate yourself to "Get Set"<br>○ Find indirect company contacts<br>○ Set-up Google alerts<br>○ Make a difference<br>○ Fill in skill gaps | ○ Act humbly competent<br>○ Confirm transferable skills<br>○ Ask for help<br>○ Perform flawlessly<br>○ Learn the process<br>○ Make a contribution |
| **HOW YOU WORK WITH OTHERS** | ○ Review previous team experience<br>○ Who's now on your team?<br>○ Beware the resistors<br>○ Where can you be at your best? | ○ Use boss's communication style<br>○ Have a get-set conversation<br>○ Get reading recommendations<br>○ Learn about job expectations, rules, culture, issues, etc.<br>○ Identify extended team<br>○ Develop a team mind-set | ○ Find a collective early win<br>○ "Manage" your boss<br>○ Take on more work<br>○ Don't get distracted<br>○ Observe the group dynamics<br>○ Find who knows who knows whom<br>○ Recognize ethical dilemmas<br>○ Look for mentors |

# POPs!

## PERSONAL ONBOARDING PLANS

**THE APPENDIX** includes several actual personal onboarding plans (POPs) prepared and used by recent graduates. You will find a variety of examples covering different jobs and using various formats.

Some are in a narrative form, others follow the suggested template, while others use checklists. Use the format that works for you. The true value is having a personal onboarding plan that leads you to take action!

Visit www.myextraordinarycareer.com for blank POP templates, additional student POPs for different career paths as well as examples of POPs from students who are currently searching for positions.

*APPENDIX* EX. 1

# PERSONAL ONBOARDING PLAN
# CONSULTING

## THE CONTEXT

I'll be starting my job as a senior consultant on October 15th, which gives me exactly four months between the date I graduate and the date I start work. Having never been a consultant before my summer internship at the company last summer, one of my priorities is to determine my skill weaknesses and set up a plan to improve them prior to my first engagement. Consulting jobs, in a way, are much like rotational programs in that a consultant is only assigned to an engagement for a relatively short period of time, and the project or role is not necessarily defined until right before it begins. This means my preparation prior to starting will need to focus more on general skill building and relationship management, since much of my success in consulting will center around identifying the industries or service lines where I can contribute most. This will also serve to best position me for a career postconsulting, if I decide a long-term career as a consultant is not for me.

APPENDIX

## CONSULTING > THE PLAN

## GET READY  *JULY 1ST THROUGH SEPTEMBER 15TH*

→ ***Update resume to highlight recent accomplishments***
Having an updated and clear resume is very important in consulting because it allows project managers to quickly assess what your skills are and whether or not you'd be able to contribute to their project.

→ ***Learn about opportunities in my industries of interest***
I'm most interested in working within two specific industry lines. To demonstrate my passion in these areas, I need to understand exactly which types of projects most suit my skills and background.

→ ***Find practitioners in these industry areas and set up brief meetings to learn about their work***
These meetings have the dual purpose of both gaining a clearer understanding of the types of projects available and demonstrating my interest in them. Each person I connect with now will be an opportunity for finding good projects that match my career goals in the future.

→ ***Develop presentation skills***
One of my most common pieces of feedback is that I need to refine my skills as a presenter, something that is particularly critical in consulting. I plan to spend time during my summer honing my skills by putting together dummy presentations and presenting in front of a mirror and people around me, which will allow me to identify my obvious weaknesses and practice in a safe environment.

→ **Start building a network of colleagues in the Los Angeles office**
I will be spending my summer in Santa Barbara, so I need to take advantage of my proximity to LA to start building critical relationships that will come in handy as I pursue a transition to this office.

→ **Start a journal of whom I know and what they do**
Since I'll be talking to a lot of new people during this time, I need to make sure I'm keeping effective track of whom I've spoken to, when I spoke to them, and what I learned from the conversations. Losing this knowledge would seriously weaken my network.

## GET SET  SEPTEMBER 16TH THROUGH OCTOBER 14TH

→ **Learn who my counselor is and start having conversations about expectations**
My counselor is basically a mentor and overseer of my progress with the firm, so a productive relationship with him is essential to having a successful career. I need to set expectations early regarding frequency of meetings and communication style.

→ **Refine my analytical skills**
Although my analytical skills are probably my strongest trait, I want to make sure I've refined my ability to use relevant tools, such as Excel, in an efficient and effective manner. I've heard the ability to be efficient is hugely important in consulting, and I need to do what I can to be ready before I start.

→ **Determine my first-year career goals**
Knowing what I want to achieve in my first year will help me get to where I need to be, so I'll articulate the steps I plan to take and where I want to be in one year. I'll go through my plans here and refine them when I first meet with my counselor after starting work.

APPENDIX

→ **Read through relevant articles and books**
There are a number of articles and textbook chapters that I feel would be helpful for my career but have not yet had time to read. I plan to determine which of these will be most useful and read them leading up to starting my job.

→ **Assess and build interpersonal skills**
As an introvert, putting myself out there and meeting people is one of the more challenging parts of my career management. I need to think hard about the best way for me to develop my skills and improve my abilities to meet and engage with others.

## GO OCTOBER 15TH ON

→ **Come in the first day with the right attitude**
Smile, be open and friendly, and welcome the opportunity to meet and be introduced to as many people as possible. The first two weeks will be filled with new faces, and ensuring my first impression is a good one will be hugely beneficial as I build my network.

→ **Act like a sponge during the first two weeks of training**
I need to absorb as much information as possible, both about the firm and the people there, getting a sense of the culture and context. Knowing how business is done there will allow me to appear competent and avoid stepping on anyone's toes.

→ **Introduce myself in person to practitioners who I've been in contact with**
Many of the conversations I'll have had over the summer will be over the phone due to my location constraint, so an in-person introduction and "thank you" should go a long way toward demonstrating my appreciation for their time.

## APPENDIX

→ ***Sit down with my counselor and formalize first-year goals***
The goals I put together in my Get Set phase will need to be discussed with my counselor to make sure he is aware of them and that they are realistic. I'll need to incorporate any feedback into my plan.

→ ***Ask questions about anything I don't know***
But be careful about to whom I direct various questions. Procedural or cultural questions are best suited for my senior manager colleagues, while questions about project opportunities or industry work can be asked of partners or other senior practitioners.

→ ***Get to know my project manager***
The manager on my first project will be my first actual boss, so gaining respect and demonstrating competence will have long-lasting ramifications. I need to start with a friendly and open-minded introduction, and then do whatever is needed on the project to show I am willing to contribute in any way to push the project forward.

→ ***Find opportunities for additional contributions to the firm***
A great way to gain additional exposure is to do eminence work, building out firm expertise in particular topics. I need to be careful, however, not to take on too much or prioritize this over project work. ☀

APPENDIX EX. 2

## PERSONAL ONBOARDING PLAN

# FINANCIAL SERVICES

| GET READY | GET SET | GO |
|---|---|---|

**WHO ARE YOU?**

*Get Ready:*
- Desire to appear informed and trustworthy
- Leverage my ability to relate to and communicate with others
- Be aware of insecurities
- Listen carefully

*Get Set:*
- Create a morning routine—rest of the day will be reactive
- Practice being comfortable about banking so that others are comfortable around me
- Professional appearance

*Go:*
- Be friendly and respectful
- Be resilient and professional
- Appear warm and approachable

**WHAT YOU KNOW**

*Get Ready:*
- Rely on EQ even more than IQ
- Think through why I've been hired
- Fill in the voids through personal study & asking for help

*Get Set:*
- Set-up Google alerts
- Read the FT, WSJ
- Tool up on financial terms
- Learn to speak about finance to friends
- Study for Series 7
- Industry context

*Go:*
- Act competently
- Ask smart questions
- Every assignment is important
- Make a contribution—find an easy way to add value

**HOW YOU WORK WITH OTHERS**

*Get Ready:*
- Co-workers & immediate team members
- Beware of resistors
- Confirm my dream assignment: sales
- Be aware of my best fit: management

*Get Set:*
- Learn boss's communication style: mid-summer lunch to discuss expectations
- Develop a team mind-set: learn with whom I will be working and what has/has not worked for them in the past

*Go:*
- Manage my first base team
- Volunteer whenever possible
- Don't get distracted
- Observe the group dynamics & culture
- Who knows who
- Recognize ethical dilemmas
- Expand my network
- Look for mentors

APPENDIX EX. 3

## PERSONAL ONBOARDING PLAN
# BRAND MANAGEMENT

**WHILE I AM SAD TO BE WINDING DOWN** my college time, I am thrilled for my next step as an Associate Marketing Manager. I came to school with the goal of changing careers from consulting into brand management at a large consumer packaged goods (CPG) company, preferably at a food company. My experience began through an internship between first and second year, where I interned in the new markets group. While I enjoyed the challenge of working on a product innovation team for the first time, I had a strong desire to understand a base marketing role, and negotiated that into my offer.

### ONBOARDING PLAN—GET READY

As I get ready for my new job in the three months before my start date, I have both my work history as well as my experiences to reflect on. The first part of my onboarding plan will include gathering all available data I have on my own professional and emotional performance. As I pack up my apartment to move back to Chicago, I can use the opportunity to gather the papers and comments from my classes, such as written responses to my work or group feedback. In one particularly useful class, "Leading and Managing Teams," I was given six pieces of constructive feedback from each of my four groupmates.

In that class, we also took an emotional intelligence test to measure our strengths and weaknesses in that area. These pieces of data will be particularly helpful to revisit now that my university time is complete and to reflect on how I can use it going forward. I also saved all of my project reviews from my previous employers, as well as written feedback from my manager during my internship. These create other data points I can use to determine what my skill set looked like earlier and consider how it may have evolved over the past two years.

I plan to use the summer to further my own learning. I have several books that I have wanted to read, particularly about leadership, that I believe will augment what I've learned and help me as I move into a leadership role at work for the first time. In particular, I've been waiting to read a set of business and leadership books written by the founder of Zingerman's, a famous deli and food company based in Ann Arbor, Michigan. I expect these books to help give me unique approaches to leading and motivating a cross-functional team, a skill set that will be important in my new role but in which I have little experience. I also have a book on the history and development of another business unit in the Chicago office. These books all serve a personal interest for me while continuing to build my knowledge about leadership and the food industry.

Finally, I will use the summer to connect with my personal support team. In my very inner circle, I am fortunate to have close friends and family members all with extensive business experience. My dad in particular has always had very good professional advice for me based on his career in finance. I also have great sounding boards in my husband, and my good friend who is going into a similar brand management role. I plan to reconnect with former managers from my previous employer. Two in particular can combine knowledge of my work history with practical advice for new MBA grads. However, one of my dear mentors from before business school had been very vocal about getting out of Chicago for better economic opportunities, advice which I clearly didn't choose to take. I have to understand that while he still could serve as a good resource, I will need to take what he says with a grain of salt. Finally, I do have good friends and advisors from my internship, and I have already started to connect with some of them to get advice on preparing for my new role.

## ONBOARDING PLAN—GET SET

Having interned with the company makes it a bit easier for me to mentally prepare and visualize what lies ahead for me, since I will be going back to a building I know well with some friendly faces around me. I am also already set on many logistical issues, like what the dress code is, and how I will travel to and from work.

This also means that many on my floor already have an impression of who I am and what I stand for as a teammate or coworker; based on my internship experience this impression should largely be positive. However, since I am expected to have this base knowledge, it will be important that I not just live up to but exceed expectations.

To get set I will also need to keep up to date on what's happening in the industry. In this instance, the benefit of going to work for a large multinational corporation is there is no shortage of news coverage. I have already been utilizing Google Alerts and reading about the company in The Wall Street Journal. I also subscribe to a handful of CPG industry newsletters like the Grocery Manufacturers Association SmartBrief, which arrives by email daily with news stories about trends and competitors. Finally, an easy and fun way to stay up to date is by walking relevant aisles at the supermarket to watch for new introductions or packaging.

Hopefully within the thirty to forty-five days before my start date I will also learn of what my first assignment will be. I would be happy and comfortable working with any of the brand teams. With the exception of my first request to work in a base role, I have not given any other specifics at this time of what I do or do not want to do. While making requests may have mitigated some risk, I feared making requests would also take away the potential upside of an exciting opportunity that comes up at the last minute. This also allows me to get excited about my assignment without creating a possibility for disappointment.

Once I have my assignment I can then get better prepared for my start date. I will be in Chicago most of the summer, so I hope that rather than speaking over the phone I can plan to meet with my new manager in person once or twice before I start. I hope to meet face-to-face once to help me make the best first impression and allow me to get a read for my new manager. This meeting will also be important to make sure we are on the same page to clarify goals and expectations for my assignment. I also plan to speak to or meet with other members of the marketing team if possible to give me additional context about the assignment, measures for success, and working with my manager. Finally, I will leverage other friends and contacts to see if they can give any additional insight about my manager and the project.

## ONBOARDING PLAN—GO!

When I start on day one, I need to be ready to make each task an opportunity to impress. One thing I learned from my internship is that managers expect finished, polished work so I can take that knowledge and know from day one not to overlook what seem like small details. I also know plans can change rapidly so it is important to approach each change or deviation as an opportunity rather than as a setback. Regardless of what else happens, the friendly faces and cheery atmosphere of the organization should help me keep a smile on my face and make a good first impression.

I plan to begin by having an open discussion with my managers about how they prefer to receive and consume information so that I can meet them on their terms. This conversation will also include any other day-to-day expectations they have, perhaps of ongoing team meetings or what times they tend to be working and when they are "offline." Our initial meetings should also outline any key dates and allow me to create an agreed-upon work plan so that my manager and I can establish on how I will go about completing my work. Finally, I plan early on to be up-front about the fact that I am open to and would appreciate any feedback, so that down the line I can ask for it on a regular basis.

Once I am back in the building, it will also be important to strengthen and grow my in-office network. For example, I have stayed in touch with many alumni and there are plenty more for me to meet. I am also one of four returning interns. Both of these groups should present safe places for me to ask questions if I need additional resources before going right to my manager. It should allow me to gather data so that I can present my manager with more solutions than questions and show that I can take initiative and be resourceful.

I know an important measure of success is being involved in office life an extracurricular activities; this is something that is taken into account for performance reviews. Therefore, I will need to immediately keep my eyes and ears open for ways to get involved, whether it is with recruiting or the office green initiative. Thankfully, the atmosphere of getting involved with activities is very similar to school and is something I've learned to balance with my day-to-day work. This is also a way to show I can successfully balance my workload while contributing to the betterment of our workplace.

# NOTES

*APPENDIX*

**EX. 4**

PERSONAL ONBOARDING PLAN
# OPERATIONS

## 4 TO 8 WEEKS BEFORE START DATE:

### GET READY — YOU

- [ ] Create POP binder. Build binder with all relevant reference materials and on-boarding plan documents
- [ ] Determine career/life balance goals. Read *How Will You Measure Your Life*, self-reflect
- [ ] Assess emotional intelligence: actively assess ability to handle stress & read others' emotions. Understand tendencies and learn to manage the tradeoffs that result from the choice I make
- [ ] Perfect listening skills: actively place myself in situations where listening is critical and challenge myself to listen more effectively
- [ ] Develop transition strategy: review *Picking the Right Transition Strategy*. Assess business situation, the organizational change, and personal change that will optimize the transition
- [ ] Discover leadership style: review *Discovering Your Authentic Leadership*
- [ ] Imagine new job: set aside 30 minutes a day to imagine the transition and the new job's responsibilities

### GET READY — COMPANY

- [ ] Research company and culture: speak with former/current employees
- [ ] Understand product/services: research new products and physically interact with them
- [ ] Expand my network: branch out and begin talking with other recruits. Forge relationships to have a support network going into the transition, people who will be going through a similar experience

APPENDIX

## GET READY — TEAM

- ☐ Who is on my team? Determine three people I trust and would approach for advice going forward
- ☐ Learn to identify and neutralize resistors. Determine who is not on my team and could potentially create friction with the transition. Learn to neutralize their feedback to minimize this friction
- ☐ Confirm assignment within team. Reach out to boss 6 weeks in advance, request a time to formally speak on the phone to have "Get Set" conversation, and confirm assignment and role within the team

## 0 TO 4 WEEKS BEFORE START DATE:

## GET SET — YOU

- ☐ Learn and address weaknesses: take feedback review during "Get Ready" and formally address weaknesses
- ☐ Find reference material to help neutralize these and better leverage strengths
- ☐ Visualize a day's activities: spend 30 minutes each day visualizing the day today, activities and mentally prepare
- ☐ Think through dress code, commute, and adjusting to the culture
- ☐ Think about how people will experience me: each week take one hour to reflect on interactions during the week, reflecting on how people experienced me and what I can do to better manage these interactions
- ☐ Begin visualizing and assessing potential quick wins: think through strengths that I have and how I might leverage these strengths easily to obtain a quick win. What will I be comparably good at? List out strengths that may lead to an early win. Review the *Quick Wins Paradox*

## GET SET — COMPANY

- [ ] Setup news feeds: begin reading everything in the news about the company. Setup Google alerts, read Tech Crunch, and watch competitors
- [ ] Prepare for group/company specifics: this group deals with sourcing and service; re-read the book *Getting To Yes* to refresh negotiation skills, locate and review material on service in the tech industry. Reach out to former professors who have experience with services to obtain additional reading material. Potential text book for reference *Service Operations 3rd Edition* by Johnston & Clark

## GET SET — TEAM

- [ ] Learn boss's communication style: determine if boss prefers e-mail/phone, formal/informal, constant/periodic
- [ ] Have "Get Set" conversation with boss: speak with boss four weeks to start date to understand goals and specifics of roles. Define communication style, team norms/rules, what people will be critical about, onboarding success, is there additional reading that would be helpful?
- [ ] Develop a team mindset based off "Get Set" conversation, define how I plan to integrate myself into the team. Determine who I will work with most closely, learn their personalities
- [ ] Learn my best fit within the team: create list of things I must focus on to fit in, creating a reference that will be important going forward

## AT START DATE, INTO FUTURE:

### GO! YOU

- ☐ Start with a smile: start and remain positive, highlight all the things I like about my job and focus on those
- ☐ Be resilient: strive to improve every day, expand my knowledge and expertise. Face disappointment with optimism (negative feedback high lights areas for improvement, create learning opportunity)
- ☐ Be proactive: continually search for ways to improve professionally and personally. Review *Fear of Feedback*
- ☐ Promote myself: without being overzealous, make sure I receive recognition when due
- ☐ Appear warm and approachable: learn and remember names... this can't be stressed enough. I am terrible with names; I must actively work on this. Say the name of the person I just met in a sentence
- ☐ Learn to demand better results: reread *Demand Better Results*- and get those ideas refreshed in my memory

### GO! COMPANY

- ☐ Identify mentors and/or advisors outside direct team: take Moleskin notebook with me to meeting, take note of other leaders names, keep track of people I admire, reach out for coffee chats, establish official mentorship. Furthermore reestablish mentor relationship with Lester
- ☐ Use corporate training as an asset: Proactively seek information about formal corporate training, expand my knowledge by taking any/all training that will be applicable
- ☐ Meld into corporate culture: be an astute observer of the culture, figure out ways that I can fit in smoothly
- ☐ Expand my network: use social events and work meetings as a way to expand my internal network

## GO! TEAM

- [ ] Manage your first boss: re-read *Managing Your Boss*. Learn to obtain great results by working with my boss
- [ ] Take on additional work, if possible: find something that nobody else seems to want to do, determine if I have a core competency in that area, and take on more work
- [ ] See if I can get an early win and support from team
- [ ] Get used to quirks: go through reps; learn the quirks of the job. Don't get overzealous; things may happen for a reason. Learn the sensitive areas of the job and what may be the exception to the rule
- [ ] Observe the group dynamics: think back to the assessment I did on my emotional intelligence. Observe how the group works together, what roles people play and how I can influence people to get things done
- [ ] Look for mentors: who in my group will help look out for me? Who can I trust? Form a relationship?

## NOTES

APPENDIX EX. 5

# PERSONAL ONBOARDING PLAN
# CONSUMER PRODUCTS MARKETING

**GET READY : JUNE/JULY**

## WHO YOU ARE

| CATEGORY | ACTIONS AND CURRENT THOUGHTS | STAKEHOLDERS INVOLVED | WEEK | TIME ALLOCATED |
|---|---|---|---|---|
| Imagine my new job and how it fits into my potential life mosaic of past, present, and future personal and professional experiences | Set aside 1 hour to spend mapping out—at this present time—what I've learned from my key "phases" in life, what I hope to learn from this upcoming new phase/job, and where I see it going in the future. This can serve as a frame of reference in the future and could/should be periodically revisited and refined. Specifically this would include: Potential Career Aspirations: General Manager, CMO, Social Entrepreneur Motivators/Values: People First, Constant Learning, Impact Personal Aspirations: Wife, Mother, Family Stages: Different jobs & rotations within each job | Self with feedback from friends | 6/25 | 90 |
| Create a professional image | Assess Physical Cues (haircut, glasses, clothes) and potentially rationalize wardrobe/go shopping! | Mother, Friend | 7/9 | 30 |
| | Solicit feedback from peers regarding communication style | Selected Classmates | 6/4 | 30 |
| | Attend a few networking sessions this summer and reflect on my "first impressions" of people and how I thought I came across | Self | 6/25 | 30 |
| Assess your emotional intelligence | Reflect on questions posed in Prof White's book. Currently, I believe my EQ is well developed but could grow in key domains (e.g., with family) and be strengthened in situations of duress | Self | 6/25 | 30 |

*APPENDIX*

## WHO YOU ARE (CONT.)

| CATEGORY | ACTIONS AND CURRENT THOUGHTS | STAKEHOLDERS INVOLVED | WEEK | TIME ALLOCATED |
|---|---|---|---|---|
| Review feedback you have received | Review 360 feedback, Past performance reviews to remind and reinforce key skills, perceptions, outages/areas of development | Self | 7/2 | 30 |
| Perfect your listening skills | Practice active listening without interrupting | Significant other, Classmates | Ongoing | 30 |

## WHAT YOU KNOW

| CATEGORY | ACTIONS AND CURRENT THOUGHTS | STAKEHOLDERS INVOLVED | WEEK | TIME ALLOCATED |
|---|---|---|---|---|
| Reflect on new job vs. old jobs | Reflect on the differences/similarities between my previous jobs and new job | Self | 6/11 | 60 |
| Match job expectations to skills | Assess skills needed for job vs. current/future skills | Self + coffee chats with current and former marketers | 7/2 | 30 |
| | Strengths Currently: Marketing, New Product Development, Interpersonal skills (ability to foster trust & relate to others), Emotional Intelligence/Self-Regulation, Team Building | | | |
| | Skills Sought include: Broader marketing and cross-functional competencies (sales, operations, etc.). Leadership: Adaptive Capacity, Leading & Empowering Others, Developing & Executing Quick Wins, Inspiring Others Through Narrative, Visioning | | | |
| Create Action Plan | Apply leadership coaching learnings and create an action plan with SMART goals to acquire or strengthen top 3 desired skills | Self | 7/9 | 30 |
| Revisit Vision | After creating an initial vision the week of 6/25 (per the "Who You Are" section), create a Plan B and other jobs/careers that could help me grow as a GM/CMO | Self | 7/2 | 60 |
| Developing leadership skills & knowledge | Create binder/dropbox of leadership articles I'd like to review over time as inspiration and reminders. Sign up for Leadership Smartbrief, HBR, and other online resources | Self | 6/18 | 30 |

## APPENDIX

## HOW YOU WORK WITH OTHERS

| CATEGORY | ACTIONS AND CURRENT THOUGHTS | STAKEHOLDERS INVOLVED | WEEK | TIME ALLOCATED |
|---|---|---|---|---|
| Who is on your team? — Understand who resistors are to different components | Lay out plan of people I know in and out of the new organization and where I stand with them (peers, mentors, advisors), as well as degree of influence. Include past managers, professors, friends, and broader support network beyond professional | Self | 7/2 | 30 |
|  | Review and lay out a more refined list of people within my new brand who can be my supporters | Self | 7/9 | 30 |
| Be aware of your best fit | Take some time to think through the business situations I've worked in (realignment, sustaining, startup). Think about what I liked or disliked and how it paired with my management style. By 7/9, should know brand assignment and take into consideration what skills are needed are in such an environment as well how to lead in such a context | Self | 7/9 | 45 |

### GET SET : JULY/AUGUST

## WHO YOU ARE

| CATEGORY | ACTIONS AND CURRENT THOUGHTS | STAKEHOLDERS INVOLVED | WEEK | TIME ALLOCATED |
|---|---|---|---|---|
| Imagine Your First Days | Write down the initial perception I want to give off at work | Self | 7/30 | 30 |
|  | Figure out logistics for how I will get to work and request first week details from HR | Self + HR | 8/20 | 30 |
| Promote yourself | E-mail select coworkers (maybe 2 or 3) to set up coffee with them in August prior to starting the job and learn more about business/team dynamics on brand | Self + coworkers | 8/6 | 30 |
| Strengthen coaching and leadership image & skills | Refine my public speaking and communication skills by connecting with staff friends to see how I can contribute my coaching skills to help guide and advise students on their career paths/burgeoning leadership skills | Self + staff + potential coaches | 7/23 | 30 |
| Thoughtfully consider first appearances/image | Get haircut while assessing wardrobe again, particularly regarding first week | Self | 8/27 | 60 |

*APPENDIX*

## WHAT YOU KNOW

| CATEGORY | ACTIONS AND CURRENT THOUGHTS | STAKEHOLDERS INVOLVED | WEEK | TIME ALLOCATED |
|---|---|---|---|---|
| Deepen knowledge of company | Pull latest Datamonitor report on industry & changing consumer behavior for brands, Set up Google alerts, Read latest 10K & Annual Report | Self | 7/30 | 60 |
| Educate yourself in job specifics | Review my city's professional organizations, alum events, industry groups to see what events I can attend to expand my professional network and skills | Self | 7/30 | 60 |
| Review resume | Revisit resume, ensure technical gaps are addressed | Self | 8/6 | 60 |
| Plan to optimize a job rotation | Part 1) Consider the adjacent businesses that contribute to the P&L of the brand beyond marketing. Think about where my brand fits within the overall division/company | Self | 8/13 | 45 |
|  | Part 2) Think about what skills/aptitudes I bring to this brand rotation. What are the key issues on the brand & how can I craft a quick win (what are the possibilities for a quick win) | Self | 8/20 | 60 |
| Anticipate your job contribution | Brainstorm where I can have impact and contribute the most for the brand. See what areas of expertise I can demonstrate | Self | 8/6 | 60 |

## HOW YOU WORK WITH OTHERS

| CATEGORY | ACTIONS AND CURRENT THOUGHTS | STAKEHOLDERS INVOLVED | WEEK | TIME ALLOCATED |
|---|---|---|---|---|
| Learn boss's communication style | E-mail future manager and inquire if phone chat or coffee chat possible to learn more about the business and connect. Get a sense for his/her communication style | Self + Future manager | 8/6 | 30 |
| Have a get set conversation w/boss | Connect with boss to learn more about business growth initiatives, challenges, team dynamics, risks ahead, people critical to business/onboarding, any recommended readings or action items. Seek understanding on where brand/business fits within the division and company (e.g., "why brand exists") | Self + Future manager | 8/13 | 30 |
| Deepen understanding of manager | Reflect on manager's style | Self | 8/13 | 45 |

## HOW YOU WORK WITH OTHERS (CONT.)

| CATEGORY | ACTIONS AND CURRENT THOUGHTS | STAKEHOLDERS INVOLVED | WEEK | TIME ALLOCATED |
|---|---|---|---|---|
| Develop a team mindset | Develop and refine "onboarding strategy" with colleagues and brand | Self (may ask a trusted advisor to review) | 8/20 | 60 |
| Evaluate corporate culture | Reflect on cultural norms and remind myself of my internship learnings. How are decisions made? How do people communicate? Meeting structure norms? | Self | 8/27 | 30 |

### GO : SEPTEMBER

## WHO YOU ARE

| CATEGORY | ACTIONS & CURRENT THOUGHTS | STAKEHOLDERS INVOLVED | WEEK | TIME ALLOCATED |
|---|---|---|---|---|
| Make a good first impression | Get enough sleep so that I start each interaction with a smile. Be open to connecting with others and try to appear warm & approachable | Self | Ongoing | |
| | Check in with manager after first week just to see how first week went. (See if there's anything I should start, stop, or continue doing) | Self + Manager | 9/10 | 15 |
| Be resilient | Remind myself that the first three months of any position is new, wrought with uncertainty, and a steep learning curve. Surround myself with allies and an encouraging "support system" who ensure I maintain personal equilibrium and authenticity to my core values | Self, Mentors/Close Friends | Ongoing | |
| Reflect upon career path | Aside from referencing the plan, thoroughly review and refine my onboarding plan again after starting work | Self | 9/24 | 60 |
| | During Thanksgiving (approximately 3 months after starting work), evaluate job and plan within context of enduring success: Happiness, Achievement, Significance, Legacy. (Nash, Laura & Stevenson, Howard. HBR. 2004. Success that Lasts.) | Self | 11/26 | 60 |
| | After three months, review brand assignment in relation to next rotation/job opportunity | Self | 12/3 | 60 |

*APPENDIX*

## WHAT YOU KNOW

| CATEGORY | ACTIONS AND CURRENT THOUGHTS | STAKEHOLDERS INVOLVED | WEEK | TIME ALLOCATED |
|---|---|---|---|---|
| Act competent | 30 min a week: Try to teach someone something that you learned/know | Self + others | Ongoing | 30 |
| Understand my brand | Read all the literature and resources I can on my brand so that I can start sharing stories about where the brand has come/use it to inspire others through narrative (vs. relying on my past brand experiences as references which detract from morale and diminish the perception of mutual acceptance) | Self | 9/3 | Hours |
| Be not afraid to ask | Reflect on list of responsibilities. Identify what I don't know and develop a learning plan including internal & external training to fill gaps/strengthen skills. Refine with manager | Self + manager | 9/10 | 45 |
| Every assignment is important | Reflect on what I am learning from this brand assignment (technical skills, managerial skills, etc.) | Self | First week of every month | 30 |

## HOW YOU WORK WITH OTHERS

| CATEGORY | ACTIONS AND CURRENT THOUGHTS | STAKEHOLDERS INVOLVED | WEEK | TIME ALLOCATED |
|---|---|---|---|---|
| Manage your first boss | Determine boss's priorities & make sure our style and priorities are aligned. Ensure that I have clear expectations of my role, responsibilities, and understanding of what success looks like for me, my manager, and the organization. (Managing Your Boss HBR 1993) | Self + manager | 9/3 | 30 |
| | Make sure I understand boss's communication style and how s/he likes to be informed. If I don't or things are off to a rocky start, course-correct immediately | Self | 9/10 | 30 |
| | Invest time getting to know admin | Self + admin | 9/3 | 30 |
| Build strong relationships with colleagues | Spend time getting to know each cross-functional and ask them about their preferred working styles, strengths, growth ideas/initiatives and seek understanding on how to help them with "our" transition as I come onboard | Self | 9/3 | Hours |

## APPENDIX

## HOW YOU WORK WITH OTHERS (CONT.)

| CATEGORY | ACTIONS AND CURRENT THOUGHTS | STAKEHOLDERS INVOLVED | WEEK | TIME ALLOCATED |
|---|---|---|---|---|
| | Biweekly: Reflect upon aspects of credibility, alignment, acceptance, contribution to see if I am bringing "relevant knowledge/skills to the organization" that are aligned with company's goals. I also need to ensure there is "mutual acceptance" and ensure that I am achieving results/making a significant contribution early on. (Hitting the Ground Running: Accelerating Executive Integration. RHR International) | Self | 9/3 | 15 |
| | Reflect and discern who I think are my potential key advisors or mentors within my team (or those familiar with the team) to see who can ensure I don't make any cultural missteps and can help help my vision, plus learning and building of a supportive team | Self | 9/10 | 30 |
| | Develop a few early quick wins at an associate level. While I don't have managerial responsibilities yet, I can still seek to discern where there are feasible opportunities to learn more about others while relying on them to contribute to the bottom-line priorities in a timely fashion. In conjunction, must make sure others feel shared achievement and are recognized for their hard work! (Quick Wins Paradox, HBR 2009) | Self | Ongoing | 60 |
| Evaluate additional work | Tendency to take on too much work so that I'm inundated but, after two months of ramping up, I should see if there's differentiating work I can take on. Coordinate with manager to see if there are any "special projects" to work on (after 3 months/upon establishing myself in strong standing) | Self | 11/5 | 30 |
| Don't get distracted | Evaluate what my manager/director's priorities are and what each cross-functional wants. Think about how I make my manager's life easier | Self | Ongoing | 15 |
| Observe the group and power dynamics around me | Reflect on decision-making process and confirm with trusted advisor/mentor at company to refine my own influence and ability to spearhead decisions | Self | 9/17 | 30 |
| Who knows who knows whom | Have 3 coffee chats a week with different people to stay connected and "in the know" about what is going on in different divisions/brands/functions | Self + Company | Ongoing | 90 |

## APPENDIX

## HOW YOU WORK WITH OTHERS (CONT.)

| CATEGORY | ACTIONS AND CURRENT THOUGHTS | STAKEHOLDERS INVOLVED | WEEK | TIME ALLOCATED |
|---|---|---|---|---|
| Recognize ethical dilemmas | If there are any issues, go to manager immediately. Do not compromise morals or values | Self + Manager | Ongoing | |
| Look for connectors (expand network) | Actively look for those who are highly connected. Review and update list of professionals that I know and my relationship with them | Self | 9/17 | 45 |
| | Join Asian American and Women's Employee Resource Groups. | Employee Resource Groups | Ongoing | |
| Look for mentors (and mentees) | Try to meet with mentor or mentee to cultivate deeper relationships and share/glean wisdom | Self | Ongoing | 30 |

## NOTES

# RESOURCES

Christensen, Clayton M., James Allworth, and Karen Dillon. *How Will You Measure Your Life?* New York: HarperBusiness, 2012.

Drucker, Peter. "Managing Oneself," *Harvard Business Review*, 77(2) (March–April 1999): 64-74.

Gabarro, John J. and John P. Kotter. "Managing Your Boss," *Harvard Business Review*, 71(3) (May-June 1993): 150-157.

George, Bill, Peter Sims, Andrew M. McLean, and Diana Mayer. "Discovering Your Authentic Leadership," *Harvard Business Review*, 85(2) (February 2007): 129-138.

Goleman, Daniel. *Emotional Intelligence*. New York: Bantam, 1995.

Kelley, Robert E. *How to Be a Star at Work: Nine Breakthrough Strategies You Need to Succeed*. New York: Crown Business, 1999.

Komisar, Randy. "Goodbye Career, Hello Success," *Harvard Business Review*, 79(2) (March–April 2000): 160-174.

Kotter, John P. and James L. Heskett. *Corporate Culture and Performance*. New York: The Free Press, 1992.

Jackman, Jay M. and Myra H. Strober. "Fear of Feedback," *Harvard Business Review*, 81(4) (April 2003): 101-107.

Jansen, Harry M., Jr. *From Values to Action: The Four Principles of Values-Based Leadership*. San Francisco: Jossey-Bass, 2011

Nash, Laura and Howard Stevenson. "Success That Lasts," *Harvard Business Review*, 82(2) (February 2004): 102-109.

Usheroff, Roz. *Customize Your Career: How to Develop a Winning Strategy to Move Up, Move Ahead, or Move On.* New York, McGraw-Hill, 2004.

Van Buren, Mark E. and Todd Safferstone. "The Quick Wins Paradox," *Harvard Business Review*, 87(1) (January 2009): 54–61.

Watkins, Michael. *The First Ninety Days: Critical Success Strategies for New Leaders at All Levels.* Boston: Harvard Business School Press, 2003.

Watkins, Michael D. "Picking the Right Transition Strategy," *Harvard Business Review*, 87(1) (January 2009): 47–53.

White, William J. *From Day One: CEO Advice to Launch an Extraordinary Career.* Upper Saddle River, NJ: Pearson Prentice Hall, 2005.

# NOTES

1. Milway, Katie Smith, Ann Groggins Gregory, Jenny Davis-Precord, and Kathleen Yazback.
"Get Ready for Your Next Assignment," *Harvard Business Review*, 89(12) (December 2011): 125–128.

2. Mallory Stark. "Creating a Positive Professional Image: Q&A with Laura Morgan Roberts," *Working Knowledge*, June 20, 2005. Retrieved August 22, 2012, from http://hbswk.hbs.edu/item/4860.html

3. Milway, Katie Smith, Ann Groggins Gregory, Jenny Davis-Precord, and Kathleen Yazback. "Get Ready for Your Next Assignment," *Harvard Business Review*, 89(12) (December 2011): 125–128.

4. Lambert, Craig. "The Psyche on Automatic," *Harvard Magazine*, November–December 2010. Retrieved August 22, 2012, from http://harvardmagazine.com/2010/11/the-psyche-on-automatic

5. Workplace Options. "Millennials Face Uphill Battle to Wow Co-Workers with Work Ethics" (press release). Raleigh, NC: Author, November 28, 2011. Retrieved August 22, 2012, from http://www.workplaceoptions.com/news/press-releases/press-release.asp?id =E42B752BC8BB4DE293E8&title=%20Millennials%20Face%20Uphill%20Battle%20 to%20Wow%20Co-Workers%20with%20Work%20Ethic

MYEXTRAORDINARYCAREER.COM

Proof

Made in the USA
Charleston, SC
08 August 2014